Marish

Mehraveh Firouz

Copyright © 2024 by Mehraveh Firouz

All rights reserved, including right to reproduce this book or portions thereof in any form whatsoever.

For information, please write to contact@firouzmedia.com

Author: Mehraveh Firouz
Illustrator: Shirin Malekesmaili
Publisher: Firouz Media

Paperback ISBN 978-1-915557-23-0
Hardcover ISBN 978-1-915557-22-3

www.firouzmedia.com/mehraveh

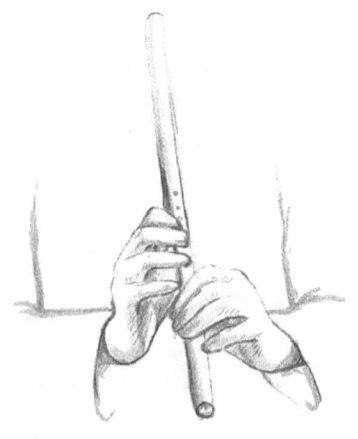

Dedicated to my mother, Lady Marish, who never left me alone, even after passing…

Chapter One

The meaning of life is that it stops.
- Franz Kafka

Mom died.

It is Tuesday, 24 January 2023, two in the afternoon Tehran time.

My brother, Farshad, is sticking the serum injection timetable on the IV pole. For mom, we have brought the hospital bed to her room. She had said she does not want to go to the hospital. She had also said that she did not want a nurse.

I am playing a piece of soothing meditation music for mom. It is playing on YouTube. It is called: Sleep softly … My brother recalls a memory and we are both in stitches. Amid the laughter, I say: Farshad, get mom's picture that was taken at Imam Reza's Shrine from her closet and hang it on the wall.

Farshad goes to get the hammer and nails.

I wash mom's face and brush her hair. The nail won't pierce the wall. Farshad says: It is on an iron beam but I'll fix it.

Mom's picture, in which she has placed one hand on her chest, is hung on the column in her room.

I put some moisturizing cream on her face. A teardrop falls from the corner of her eye. I caress her. I tell her I love her. I say: It's all right mom, we're just making the bed … Are you upset mom? Farshad, mom is crying!

Her tears change into a lump in her throat. She whimpers like a small child, her bottom lip quivers, and her eyes shut.

Farshad, mom's not breathing … mom, mom…

I scream … I beg her … I connect the oxygen tank.

Farshad presses her chest … Mom, mooom … But there is no life left in mom.

Farshad bangs his head against the wall. Several times. Involuntarily. The whole room is spinning.

Call the emergency services. Call the emergency services.

They arrive in under ten minutes.

One of them says: "It's over…" Another one says: "Open the windows to keep the room cool until the body removal vehicle arrives." A third one is less cold-hearted: "May she rest in peace … May God give you patience…"

They are talking about my mother. Mom was gone.

"Farshad, tell them to leave … Tell them to leave mom's room."

"This way sir … Thank you … This way please…"

Mom's bosom is warm. I take refuge in it. I take her entire volume in my arms. I don't know what has happened. She had asked me to play her only reed music. My hands are trembling. I look for it:

Reed music by Master Hasan Kasaei...

The room is cold. We dress her in the clothes she likes; the same ones she always used to say were soft and light ... I put her favorite perfume on her. The sound of the reed playing fills the house. Farshad pulls the white sheet over mom's face. I won't leave the room. If I stay with her and take her in my arms, this nightmare will end.

My brothers arrive one by one. Afshar comes. He takes my hand and tells me in a trembling voice: "Mehraveh ... Please. For mom's sake, come out of this room..." He is still unable to swear by anything other than the life mom no longer has.

Mehran's back is bent in two. He cannot stand straight. He strikes his knees and says: "The day I was afraid of is here ... It's all over ... We're doomed...

I have never seen him in such a state before.

I return to mom's room. I pull back the white sheet. Mom looks prettier. Mom hasn't flinched. Mom has humiliated death. She did not believe in weakness and meltdowns. Her head was always held high. And now, we, her children, were bent in two. I caress her entire being.

Mom, death is so powerful ... I can't get up ... My illustrious mom ... My strong mom ... My kind mom...

There is no escape. A profound sorrow weighs down on my heart like a mountain range. I feel a banging against my heart like an iron mace. I have trouble breathing.

The doctor sits on mom's chair. Exactly where she used

to have breakfast every day. Calmly, he stamps a sheet of paper. Deceased. The sound of the stamping is released like a bullet out of death's hunting rifle. The collective screaming of birds echoes in the darkness of the forest.

> They took mom.
> She went alone…
> She will be buried tomorrow morning.

Chapter Two

The pupil dilates in darkness and in the end finds light, just as the soul dilates in misfortune and in the end finds God.

- Victor Hugo

I scroll through YouTube. I come across an animation and click on it. It is a very simple animation but has had many views. With a few examples, it proves that there is no god. I feel curious. I visit their channel. I watch more animations. I read the comments. They have recommended a few books to read. I get the books. I read. It's true. There is no other world! It makes me happy. So, there's nothing happening on the other side! Whatever there is is right here. I had also read about various other theories years ago but was not convinced. This simple animation showed me in a few minutes that I have been fooled and there is no god. I read more scientific articles and every day I believe more that death is the shared destination of all existence in the universe. The rest of the stories are merely legends and mirages and everything ends with death.

It is frightening. That this is all there is! That it ends! Is this it? And no more!

I think to myself, I don't have much time left! There is so much I haven't experienced yet … There are so many places out there that I haven't seen yet. New flavors I had to taste … Get going! Time is running out! This is it! And then the end!

I also feel somewhat appeased! I think to myself, so there is no blame and judgment either. There are no limitations. It will all end here and that's that! So, there is no this is right and this is wrong! No more constraints! Every person can set their own boundaries, or be boundless … There will be infinite choices.

Needless to say, all hell will break loose. So what! But no, we can't have that! Freedom at what price? There will be no peace and security left. It will be the law of the jungle! In the jungle, however, the animals are living their lives, freely. Still, we humans have also destroyed that…

Despite feeling lost in my labyrinthine thoughts, I can't live without laws and walls. I set myself a rule:

My boundaries of freedom extend to the point where they don't interfere with others.

And my life is turned upside down without me realizing it.

I will not settle for less. I am fearless. I make my list, uncompromisingly; lists of my wishes and aspirations. I create the images in my mind. My wishes come true. I don't notice them. They don't seem like much. I keep wanting more. I don't remain idle for a moment. I work over sixteen hours a day. I turn the wheels. I cannot stay put.

I meet with successful individuals. I write the stories of outstanding people. I interview them. Ask them how they found out what they want in life. Where was the turning point in their life and at what point did they discover themselves? What did they suffer? Are they happy with their journey?

I search for my raison d'être in other people. My image of myself is not solid. It's fluid. It's not clear. Who am I? I stand facing the mirror. I see a stranger. I cannot say who I am in three words or a sentence. I feel like a thousand characters…

I take all my thousand personas and emigrate. I obtain a PhD scholarship from Laval University. French Literature. I study. I write. I experience diverse professional activities. My books are published in different languages.

That the clock is ticking eats away at me like a corrosive substance. Get moving!

I travel. From one end of the world to the other. I feel a hole inside me. Something's missing. I don't have a moment's peace. I think something fundamental is missing from my existence. No one knows how I feel on the inside. An inner accuser is always present there. Why does it always wave its stick in the air? After all, I have never spared any effort!

What's wrong with me?

Mom says: "Sweetheart, I think enough is enough …

You've lived to your heart's content. And you have

everything you've ever wished for! Choose yourself a home somewhere in this world, settle down, and enjoy your life. Stay put now. A pigeon cannot make a nest alone! You must have a mate…"

A companion makes me feel restless. I cannot go the distance. I'm happier alone. I hope for a miracle. For something to happen and change everything. But I don't know what. I only know that I'm caught in the cycle of events.

***

I'm in my office. They connect a call to my extension. The ring of the phone unsettles me. Someone asks me to change their contract. I feel ambushed. I don't accept his file. I hang up. I waive the advance payment which is a significant amount.

Why has a simple issue enraged me so? Why are my hands shaking? My lips are dry! Something inside me is screaming. I can no longer evade myself. I must cure this ailment. The wound has split open. This suffering is a warning. I can no longer close my eyes on it.

***

It is the year of the modern plague; COVID-19!

Determined, I join the online therapy session with a cup of coffee. Dr. Neda asks a few questions
- I think my problem is anxiety.
- What makes you feel anxious?

It's like sitting in front of a mirror. I'm facing myself, with no distractions. She looks at me deeply. Her eyes make me feel safe; like a still ocean that has put behind many storms. Skilfully, she stops me from evading the questions.

At first, it seems like an ordinary therapy session with no special upshots on the horizon. Only a few moments have elapsed since the start of the session. I am crying! This outburst of emotion is out of character for me. I think this inner state of disarray had scrambled to emerge time and again on numerous occasions but I had put out the fire. These painful moments uncover the ambiguous corners of my soul.

Dr. Neda puts her finger on old wounds; the same ones I had entrusted to the archives, ignored, or was unaware of.
- Will you take my hand?
- No!

I resist. In my mind, I'm shielding myself. I don't want her to open the doors I had shut one after the other. I don't want her to peel my wounds layer by layer; all my walls would collapse! How would I be able to protect myself out there with a delicate, fragile skin? And yet, Dr. Neda had pulled back the curtains.

I say I have lost the meaning of life.
- Whether you decide to climb up the Himalayas or not, it won't change the essence of the mountain range but it may either relieve your anxiety or distress you more because this is the meaning you've created for your life – to open your eyes in the morning and wake up to climb up there. Do you think these ascensions make

your identity?
- It's a way of life. You take no options off the table. You don't choose or decide what you want. It's easier because you still own everything, all options are open to you, and you can please yourself.
- But this is not a courageous life. You have everything and nothing! Because you don't have a destination. Once you've set out your values, you will have feathered your nest…

***

I walk to the beach. Several seagulls approach me and fly away again. I feel a ringing in my ears. I hear the whistling.

I don't know who you are … I don't know whether you exist or not … If you're there, show yourself … If you're there, show me the way; I am lost…

The sun is setting. Its fiery orange color is spread across Lake Ontario. I pick up my cell phone to take a picture. I see consecutive numbers:

Walk in your own strength, live with your own truth, and believe. Your angels are watching over you. Your angels bring you love and protection…

I think, do angels exist?

Chapter Three

Every night, when I go to sleep, I die. And the next morning, when I wake up, I am reborn.
  - Mahatma Gandhi

I speak to mom on the phone. She says she dreamt of the angel of death last night.

I was cooking. I turned around and saw a very tall person nearly reaching the ceiling hovering above me in the kitchen. It was very beautiful. It wore a long, black robe and had very bright green eyes; they also emanated a bright green sparkle. He said to me I had come to take you but you've been given a little more time ... I woke up. I looked everywhere but there was no one in the house...

I tell her it's a good omen mom! There is a good interpretation. You will have a long life. But I feel anxious inside.

Mom doesn't want us to change our plans and go to any trouble on her account. She says I'm fine. Look after yourselves!

Even so, I buy a ticket straight away and leave for Iran.

Mom does not want to go to the hospital. She shirks all doctors, medication, and syringes. She says I don't want them to tell me that I have an incurable disease and then I won't be able to live comfortably. I'm fine. Don't worry about me.

I speak to the person in charge of the clinic on the phone.
- Yes, please. A blood test and full check-up. Fine. I'll see you at ten o'clock tomorrow morning at home.

Mom has laid the breakfast table. Tomato omelette. Fresh sangak flatbread with sesame seeds on both sides. Paneer. Walnuts. Dates. Fresh basil. Raw honey. Fresh kaymak. Fig jam. The scent of freshly brewed tea with cardamom, rosehip, and cinnamon.

She drops a piece of saffron rock candy in her tea estekan.
- Mehi, I'm fine! Why should I have a blood test?
- Mom, it's just a routine check-up. Don't worry about it. It's not painful! I laugh.

Mom loves life, even though she hasn't had an easy one. Soaking in the joys of a cuppa seems to open the gates to a peaceful world for her. Drinking a cup of tea with mom is as soothing as a few therapy sessions.

The test results arrive. Mom's fine. A few days pass. Everything is all right but mom seems tired. She says I have no strength.

Dr Alizadeh, her doctor, comes. He takes her blood pressure and prescribes her a strengthening serum and vitamins. He has always been a lifesaver for mom. When she contracted COVID, he saved her life.

We redecorate the house for mom and rearrange the furniture. We do the spring cleaning and buy new sofas. Mom says I could've lived with my old ones…

I change the burned-out light bulbs. She had asked for a water purifier to be installed several times and I had procrastinated. Two days pass. Mom's not well.

We test her for COVID. She has contracted it for the third time despite the jab. It's less serious this time. I nurse her.

As she wakes up first thing in the morning, her entire body begins to shake. I have never seen mom in this state. I contact her nurse urgently and she arrives in the blink of an eye. A cold sweat is sitting on mom's forehead and her whole body is shaking. As soon as she feels calmer, she addresses her nurse with a smile: I was dying there for a minute…

I ask her not to be stubborn and go to a specialized clinic. She accepts at last.

The specialist is a kind man. She asks mom a few questions and says yes, it's COVID again! He checks the test results and says everything seems all right! But it's best to have a scan as well.

After the tests, I ask mom to sit in a wheelchair and I ask the doctor to give the results of the scan to me only. I go into his office.

- Unfortunately, large cancerous masses are seen in the uterus, ovaries, and intestines. A large part of the liver is also affected ... It's most probably a lymphatic metastasis ... She must be hospitalized immediately ... We need more tests ... It's too late ... It's too late...

***

I leave his office with a fake smile but my eyes speak to mom. My eyes can never lie. I can't hospitalize her there. I must take her home, to her peaceful haven. Just like the time when I was going through a bad patch and she turned hell into heaven for me with her simple words. I had to cook her a delicious meal; it had to be a labor of love, just like she always calmed us down with a warm plate of scrumptious snacks. And I had to quietly convince her to do more tests. Just like when I had gone bankrupt and she bought me cream cakes ... Get up girl! You created all of this and you can do it again! Get up! There's no such thing as loss! Put your hands on your knees and get up! And she had soothed my suffering with a cream cake, a cup of hot tea, and a few words. That day, I understood that being healed did not mean eliminating the loss but that the loss and suffering could no longer control me. But what am I going to do now mom?

I tell her you are in rude health mom! They just need to do a few more tests to set our minds at rest. You are tired now ... We'll come back later.
- Yes, please take me away from here quickly. Please ... She begs like a kid.

I manage to swallow the lump in my throat. It's Thursday

night. I take mom home. She takes a bath and says she wants some mincemeat kebabs with saffron rice. I order a takeaway. She slips into her comfortable clothes.

I get into the shower. I cry. My mother has cancer and doesn't know it. I recall what she used to say. She always said:

I'm afraid I might get cancer and become dependent on care. I'm afraid I might get colon cancer like my father! Don't take me for tests … They'll tell me I have cancer and then I won't be able to live comfortably…

All her worries have come true. She has had cancer all these years and we didn't know it. She's been living with cancer without even being in pain … But why were there no symptoms! Why were the test results good! This damned COVID is to blame. COVID has fuelled the fire of all miseries. I cry in the shower and remember mom's dream. It has come true…

I'm sitting in Balzac's Cafe in Toronto. My heart is set on fire as I recall these memories. I have my headphones on. *Gloomy Sunday* by Diamanda Galás is playing:

> Sadly one Sunday
> I waited and waited
> With flowers in my arms
> All the dreams I had created
> I waited 'til dreams,
> Like my heart, were all broken

The flowers were all dead
And the words were unspoken
The grief that I knew
Was beyond all consoling
The beat of my heart
Was a bell that was tolling

Saddest of Sundays

Then came a Sunday
When you came to find me
They bore me to church
And I left you behind me
My eyes could not see
What I wanted to love me
The earth and the flowers
Were forever above me
The bell tolled for me
And the wind whispered, "Never!"
But you I have loved
And I'll love you forever

Last of all Sundays

My eyes are wet. This is not Iran. Nobody comes to ask you what's wrong. I don't want anyone to see my tears ... Why am I even worried about other people! Damn my labyrinthine thoughts...

I must be strong. This time, it is mom who needs my support. At last, I manage to convince her to go for more tests. She makes me promise not to hospitalize her. I reassure her. She clings to me like a hurt child before the CT scan and MRI. She cries. Even drinking water and liquids before the tests makes her suffer. She says: I'm not well ... Take me away from here...

I can't stop the tears ... I beg her to endure it for a while...

- It'll be over soon ... It'll be over in a minute mom...

The doctor stares at the test results and then at the monitor in front of him. He looks back at the papers. He is oblivious to my restlessness. I'm chewing on the skin of my thumb. It breaks. It bleeds. I make a fist.

The cancer cells have progressed too far ... It is as if I'm in the classroom and he is talking about the Ottoman Wars. It has now metastasized to the liver ... Stage 4 ... There is a build-up of ascites fluid around the organs ... We must begin the chemotherapy ... You must tell your mother the truth so that she can decide. Chemotherapy prolongs the patient's life with more suffering ... It's far too late ...

I'm nailed to the ground. I take the file. It's like failing school. I put my hands under my arms, lift myself up from the chair, and leave the room. I keep repeating to myself: I'm not wobbly...

Why haven't I installed the damned water filter yet? Mom doesn't like to get so much mineral water! I must take her dress fabric to the tailors. It is a light and soft fabric. Just the way she likes it … It has a black background covered in colorful butterflies. My steps are not wobbly … There is so much left to do … Get on with it woman! Pull yourself together … Pull yourself together…

I bring mom out in a wheelchair. Helia, my niece, is waiting for us in the car. Mom sits in the backseat. It's the Woman, Life, Freedom movement. There is a feeling of curfew across the city. Everywhere is full of security forces.

I ask what would you like for lunch mom? She wants liver.

Helia is at the wheel. She glares at me. It means no! It means it's not good for her, auntie!

I say, OK mom. There's a really good restaurant nearby; it has tables in the garden. Shall we go there?

She says let's go! Helia is here too. We'll have fun!

Helia presses her lips together and says:

- Sure grandma! I'll take you somewhere cool!

Mom is happy. We pretend as if nothing has happened and we are happy too. Two kids selling fortunes approach us. We buy them food. One of them says I want barbecued chicken, auntie.

I say, sure. We buy him and his friend everything they want. He holds out his pack of poem fortunes at me. I say I don't want my fortune told. He gives mom a flower.

We go home. I brew some tea.

The nausea starts.

The pain starts.

Feeling sick.

She vomits.

Mom says I've been like this since COVID.

My darling mom. She pretends that everything is just fine, as always! But nothing is fine mom … It is unbelievable and nothing is fine. Little by little, I trickle away on the inside. I have come to depend on mom more than ever before.

My brother and family members have heard the news. They hide their tears from mom in total disbelief. This typhoon has turned our home upside down for seven days now! One person sticks their head in their cell phone. Someone else goes to the car park under the pretext of having left something behind in the car and doesn't return for some time. Another one keeps busy pouring the tea.

The news of mom's illness seems to have brought us closer together. We are in a state of countdown! Every second counts. I cannot tell whether mom has suspected anything of our behavior or not! She says I've been wanting to travel really badly for the last few days. Somewhere lush … We'll go north with Mehi when I'm better, or maybe we'll go to Ardabil. I'll bring back feteer, paneer, and pennyroyal from there. What's the matter with me? I have morning sickness like expectant mothers. And she laughs.

Mom never spoke of her wishes. Everything is different these days. There does not seem to be much time left to waste on standing on ceremony. Is it possible that she has guessed?

Shahpur can barely swallow the lump in his throat and leaves the sitting room.

I say I will order them online mom, until you are better...

I have barely finished speaking when we hear Shahpur's voice from the bedroom: "Send it to me tomorrow morning with the first freight. Thank you my friend. I'll personally pick it up from Azadi terminal. Fresh paneer please ... Make it the best..."

Mom feels ashamed. She says I shouldn't have mentioned it ... I've put you to too trouble!

Mom has great self-esteem. Her language of love has always been one-sided, offering her unconditional love to her children and family without expecting anything back in return. And now, when she wishes for something out loud, we all want to make it happen, heart and soul, no matter how small.

Mom, it's too late ... it's too late ... it's not fair...

The following day, all the goodies from Ardabil were on the kitchen table, from black sesame seeds, fresh unsalted paneer, honey, and kaymak, to black halva, and pennyroyal... Mina has baked fateer bread; both simple fateer and also with halva.

Mom says my daughter-in-law and son have brought Ardabil home to me. And she looks at them with a deep love.

The taste of the warm, freshly baked fateer takes me back to my childhood years, when my eldest paternal aunt baked hundreds of fateers stuffed with halva in a traditional oven, as well as fresh unsalted paneer, and brought it for us. Mom really liked auntie. She used to say my own eyes have deceived me, but never auntie. This one time, when she was sitting at the prayer mat, she told mom: "Marish, I'm on my last legs now. Sometimes, I just want an estekan of chay but don't have the energy to get up and get it. I'm ashamed of my children ... I don't want to put them to any trouble. If only God would forgive me and take me as soon as possible ... And a week after that conversation, she had left this world...

I ask myself, what has happened to our women that they are so afraid of dependence and deny themselves the love of those around them!

I take mom's medical records and leave Iran on a short trip. I go to the American Hospital in Dubai for a second opinion: for a grain of hope...

With one voice, they all say:
- Stage 4! Stage 4! Chemotherapy!

The cancerous cells had traveled in mom's body. From the uterus. From the ovaries. From the colon. And now the liver metastases...

Now I know what it means when they say "your arms are longer than your legs"[1]. It means me!

I stand in front of the chocolate shelves like a mourner. The palette of lemon, mango, and strawberry flavored German bonbons that mom loves to have with her tea ... Mom loves chocolates. It kills me to pick up those few packets of sweets. I console myself: Everything will be all right...

I set eyes on a white shirt and trousers with pink spring blossoms. Soft and light. Just the way mom likes it. The

---

1. It means coming back with your tail between your legs

back of my throat feels bitter. There is a flask next to them with small pink blossoms too. I take it.

***

Mom wears her presents. She says: Ahh! It's so soft…

I bring her a cup of tea. Just then, Kiana calls. I relax. Mom feels better every time she talks to Kiana. She comes alive. Kiana, my only sister, emigrated to the UK over fifteen years ago and never looked back. And all these years, with every step mom took, she never failed to say: I miss Kiana … I wish Kiana was here … They saw each other during trips. In Istanbul. In Dubai. In Toronto. Followed every time by restlessness at the airport when saying farewell…

I use the opportunity to take a video of mom; to remember. I choke. Everything has taken on the taste of "last things". Last new clothes. Last chocolates. Last presents. Last voices … I calm myself down.
- I'm fine darling. Even better than before. See how light I am on my feet! I can walk easily. My leg is a little swollen but it will be all right. I'll come to see you soon.

Tell me what you want me to bring from Iran. I want to come and stay with you for a month…

She speaks with her usual optimism and they both avoid the truth.

After the phone call, she tells me: When Kiana and Farshad ask about me, tell them that I'm fine … They're far away and will find it difficult. Homesickness is heartbreaking…

In a choked voice, Kiana sends me a voicemail: "Have you told mom?" "No! Not yet!"

I can barely swallow my saliva.
- Mom!
- Yes sweetheart?

I put the words together at painstakingly and talk to her about her illness.

She smiles and says: I knew right away at the clinic that day, you were hiding my illness from me. I saw it in your eyes. It's fine sweetheart. I'll think about it and let you know of my decision about the chemotherapy.

She never flinched. My strong mother…

That night, she went to sleep a few hours later than usual.

As I was making breakfast in the morning, she said I thought a lot last night. I'm not scared. My only chagrin is that I can't let go of my children. It's so hard. Last night, I dreamt I was in a vast, green expanse and I was peaceful … And she added, I have made my decision; I'll stay home!

She had a smile on her face. Determined. Calm. Collected. With boundless self-confidence as usual. She said I don't want my body to be changed. I have lived my life and I will trust myself into God's hands like every other time. Whatever He wants will happen. I have never begged for life.

Mom chose how to face death with her usual strength.

The children come one by one and take mom's medical records away in search of a piece of hope! But they return after a few days, dejected, and place the file, which has now turned into my concave mirror, next to the vase on the buffet…

Mom has only just learned to send voicemail on WhatsApp and make video calls.

- Mehi, I'm not sure who has tampered with my cell phone! I want to send the children a voicemail. The two ticks won't turn blue. There's just a small circle that keeps spinning! Nothing goes through!

I say I'll fix your phone mom. I don't say that the government has tampered with all our cell phones and filtered them!

She falls asleep and wakes up with the drip in her arm. She says, I dreamt that someone gave me a pomegranate. They said, you'll get better if you eat this.

I bring her a pomegranate. She looks at me and tells me to interpret her dream instead of doing such things.

I want to burst into tears but I smile and say sure. Pomegranate is a symbol of health…

Mom is anxious. Mom is restless. Mom was never

anxious before, or at least didn't show it.

Helia brings her some propranolol tablets. Some time passes. Mom feels calmer. Afterwards, whenever she felt restless she'd say, Mehi give me Helia's tablets. I don't feel well.

She wants some fresh air. She's restless. It is eleven o'clock at night. We walk to Gheitarieh Park. She says, let's go back. I have a backache. I want to lie down.

I am holding her hand. She squeezes mine a little every time the pain intensifies. I absorb her pain but there is nothing I can do. I am familiar with how every single one of her knuckles feels. It is life itself. Mom never aged.

- Mom, would you like a fruit punch?
- Yes, but get me a small one.

I stop outside the fruit punch shop. They're closing down. They've cleaned their equipment. He says, we're not taking any more orders.

I say just a small one for mom ... I choke and can't finish my sentence.

Straightaway, he says of course. I'll make you one right now.

There is a flower shop next to the fruit punch shop. Mom loves narcissus and tuberose. She says flowers are not as fragrant as before.

I look at mom in the car and wave at her.

I go into the flower shop.

- Do you have fresh, scented narcissus and tuberose? I want them for my mom.
- Yes, I have some very good ones. I was closing up and

going home. This will be my last take of the night...
I give mom the flowers. She smells them and says they're so fragrant.

I get the fruit punch. He has made two cups.

He says: I'd like to treat you to an extra one. Be my guest! May you be in good health!

Mom only takes a couple of sips...

I say, mom, he treated us to one.

She says, may he be in good health...

***

Mom is getting weaker by the day. She cannot walk. Slowly, she loses her ability to speak.

Everything she has been given is taken from her one by one but mom won't stop being thankful. She doesn't flinch and still loves the smell of freshly brewed tea. We spoon-feed her the tea. Her feet are swollen. We massage them with sea salt.

In private, she makes recommendations to every child in line with their lives and shows them her appreciation. For every drop of water I give her, she says: Ah ... that was really good ... Thank you God...

Mom thanked God for her aches and pains and I cried secretly. She thanks the doctor who is visiting her at the height of her pain and suffering and tells him: Thank you doctor. You have calmed me down...

She is not well. Her nurse arrives. She sets up the IV drip to deliver the bone-strengthening and anti-anxiety drugs. She says, I love her like my own mother. This woman has magnanimity…

Mom had asked me to make her favorite dish.
- Mehi, will you make me some rice with noodles?

I know it is not good for her. I know she can only eat a few spoonfuls. It makes her nauseous. I say: Sure mom.

She wants to try all the tastes of life again before going.
- Use lots of noodles and little rice.
- Sure mom.

I make great rice with noodles. With great care and patience. A labor of love. With lots of raisins. Butter. Caramelized onions. Just the way she likes it.

It's sundown.
- Are you better mom? The noodle rice is ready.

She eats a couple of spoonfuls. She looks at me and smiles. She knows I have put my all into it. I, who haven't cooked in years.

It's morning. It's snowing. I push her bed to the window and draw back the curtains. I help her to lie facing the window. She doesn't resist. She always used to say draw the curtains sweetheart. The others can see inside the house.

She places one hand over the other. Mom means peace. Even when she is sick. Even if her eyes are shut. I watch her. My heart calms down.

The snow has stopped. The sun shines a little from behind the clouds. The rays are shining on her hands.

I make breakfast. She had said she felt like halim and lentils. I place a few pillows behind her to make her sit up comfortably. Her stomach is swollen due to the damned ascites fluid and she can barely move. I play her favorite Azari program; the everyday life of an Azari couple who cook in the traditional way in the hillsides of the Caucasus Mountains. The woman is making spinach bureks. Her husband has gathered wildflowers to brew tea. He is chopping logs for firewood. The roosters are crowing loudly and there is the crackling sound of the burning firewood. Mom is just watching and she has only eaten a spoonful of the halim.

I curse myself for not taking her to Baku earlier! Why did I delay the Baku trip! She wanted to travel to Azerbaijan and visit the land of her ancestors.

I had asked Farshad who lives in Canada to return to Iran quickly. He had arrived a week earlier. The night he arrived, he held mom in his arms until dawn and didn't let go of her for a moment.

Mom tells me: Mehi, I know my time is short … I just want to see all my children in one place together one more time before I go…

Her words sound like the nail in her coffin. What did I possibly have in my repertoire to say faced with her authority despite her affliction!

There are only a few days left until Mother's Day.

I say: Mom, it's Mother's Day today! All the children will be here tonight...

That night, mom held everyone in her arms.

She looks at us intensely; like someone who is standing at an airport gate and saying goodbye forever. She does not speak. She just watches ... It is as if she wants to consign something to memory...

I stay by her side all throughout the night. She is in pain. Her anguish increases closer to sunrise. Her dying moment is here. My heart is on fire. Everything progresses according to her wishes. Is it even possible for someone to choose their time of demise!

She had said she would see her children and go!

No matter what I did, she was inconsolable. She was agitated. Even the morphine no longer worked. Finally, I was resigned.

I said, mom, you always trusted in God. You used to say my life was hanging by a thread but it never snapped ... Trust in God now ... Say hello to God ... Let go of us ... Don't worry about us ... Take God's hand ... I sobbed and caressed her...

At that moment, mom stopped moaning. She placed her right hand on her chest and stared straight ahead. She said: Salam O Imam Reza ... And repeated: Salam O Imam Reza ... Salam...

She kept shaking her head. In a louder voice, she said: He is taking my life...

- Mom, give Him your hand … Don't be scared! Don't be worried! Trust in God like always…

I sobbed relentlessly. My mother was losing her life…

She turned to me upset and said: Don't cry … Don't cry now! She said salam one more time and closed her eyes.

Mom was in a coma.

I had to decide whether we should take her to the hospital or take care of her at home as per her wishes. The doctors could not give a date for how long she would be in a coma.

I sat next to her and took her hands. I said, mom, I promised you I wouldn't take you to the hospital.

With the help of Dr Alizadeh, we quickly furnished her room with the hospital equipment, from a hospital bed and anti-decubitus mattress to a home oxygen concentrator and…

I confide in her every day. I miss the sound of her voice. I think mom has forgotten that she is the light of our life. Why won't she wake up?

My favorite author, Romain Gary, ended his life with a bullet after his wife died. In a note, he wrote: "D-Day. No connection with Jean Seberg … I have at last said all I have to say." He added: "I had a lot of fun. Good-bye and thank you."

Freud said: "The goal of all life is death". When he detected a growth in his mouth and contracted leukoplakia cancer, he suffered much pain and agony. In the end, he chose a self-inflicted death. Virginia Woolf filled her pockets with stones and drowned herself in the River Ouse in Rodmell…

Mom had asked for the nurse not to come. We looked after her. Afshar, my brother, had brought her white custom-embroidered sheets. We bathed her in her wheelchair and combed her hair. I applied a special moisturizer made from raw honey on her hands.

I send Mehri a message to come. Mehri is my classmate from my undergraduate course; a kindhearted friend who comes if I send her just one message even if I haven't seen her for years. I solicit Mehri's help to deliver mother's belongings to those who may need them.

I take mom's clothes one by one, smell them, kiss them, and say goodbye to mom.

I see her swimming costume. It throws me back to the day she wore it for the first and last time; on my insistence that the hot spring was good for her aching legs. I place the swimming costume on my eyes and my laughing and sobbing breaks me up profoundly. Afshar sees me.
- What are you laughing at?
- Look at mom's swimming suit…

He presses his lips together and says: I've also sorted out mom's handbags.

Helia had asked me for one of mom's shades that we had bought together in Turkey. I put it to one side for her. She had said, auntie please give me grandma's estekan too; the only one she drank tea in.

I hold the butterfly dress in my arms and keep it.

O mom … My traveler of no return…

Ten days have passed and mom has not woken up. Nevertheless, I feel less anxious. I still talk to Dr. Neda. She also indicates that I feel stronger and calmer…

I always went to mom's room in the early mornings. I opened the curtains and said good morning to her. I changed her clothes and sheets and gave her a face wash. I put on perfume for her and connected the feeding drip. I moisturized her throat with a mixture of warm water and raw honey, and then a few teaspoonfuls of warm water … I caressed her. I kissed her hands, massaged them, and spoke to her.

That morning, the snowfall was heavy. Everywhere was

white. I went to mom's room and opened the curtains. Like every other day, I said: Good Morning mom ... That's when the voice came. I couldn't believe my ears ... Mom answered me...

- Good Morning love...

Electrified, I turn around and say: Mom! Are you talking, mom? Are you awake?

God only knows how much I had missed the sound of her voice...

- Yes, sweetheart ... I'm awake ... I'm talking...

Her face was even more beautiful, like an angel.

I grew wings. It was Thursday. The doorbell rang. I was exhilarated that one more person would also see mom talk.

It was Shahpur. He says he was deep in thought at the wheel when he had an accident. He had left the car at the garage and came straight here to visit mom.

Excited, I say no worries! Come ... Come, mom is talking.

Mom always spoke in Azari to us. Ever since she has woken up, however, she speaks in Persian in a childish tone: Pure. Pleasing. Sweet...

Mom's manner of speaking has changed. My heart melted at the sound of her voice. I was on cloud nine. I ask, are you in pain mom? She says, no! I'm fine. I have no pain. I just want some tea.

Shahpur says: Just ask for my life mom ... sure, sure...

Mom looks at him and speaks in that same sweet tone: I just love those gorgeous eyes...

Shahpur's green eyes are filled with tears and a smile

spreads over his face.

I bring her freshly brewed tea. She only takes a sip. She looks at me and my brother with boundless love, as if she has returned from a long trip.

Amazingly enough, she talks about everything that we have done.

- Thank you for not taking me to the hospital and caring for me at home without a nurse ... It's good that you changed the bed ... Just remove this pillow! It's too big. My head's not comfortable. I kept telling you but you couldn't hear me...

I stand there with rounded eyes.

- Mom! You were in a coma then. How do you know all this? Could you see me?

She just smiled kindly and looked at us.

- Your father came to fetch me and took me with him ... I was so scared ... I wasn't sure what was happening and where we were going. He showed me everywhere. He showed me my new home. I feel at ease now. Imam Reza came into this room twice. I said to him I want to go back. He said why do you want to go back? I said: I'm worried about my children. I asked for a little more time...

With her thumb and index finger, she showed that they had given her this much time. Then, she turned to me and said: It's time now.

- I don't understand mom! What does it mean that you have a little time?

Mom kept talking in her pure, childish tone, like a two-year-old. I had never seen her like that before. These must be hallucinations or the effects of the medication. Once again, she indicated a very small amount with her thumb and index finger. Like little children when they say just a little bit…

She had seen me give away all her belongings, clothes, and handbags!

- Were you upset mom?
- No. You did well! They all went to good homes! I don't need anything anymore!

In my total disbelief, she was aware of everything…

I called all the family to come quickly because mom had woken up. Everyone arrived in less than an hour.

The light of our home had been lit. Mehran had brought barberry rice with chicken from the big bazaar in Tehran. It was like a wedding in our house.

I couldn't keep still. I had a mother again. Mom was a genteel, powerful, and dignified woman with high self-esteem. She always watched us with pride. I had never seen her complain about a problem. I always envied her patience and perseverance.

One by one, everyone went to mom. She would tell each one a heart-warming sentence that served their lifestyle and her offspring would leave the room with tears of joy.

I wanted to take her some fruit juice when I heard her say to Mehran: Why were you crying by my bedside? I wasn't unwell! I kept saying don't cry! I'm fine! But you wouldn't hear me. You are my king. I'm very happy with you. I don't have the heart to see your tears…

Freud wrote: "A man who has been the indisputable

favorite of his mother keeps for life the feeling of a conqueror."

***

It was a miracle. Mom had no pain. She was feeling well. The doctor and ultrasound specialist came. In awe, they said this is truly a strong woman! How has she managed to last! None of her organs work! Mom, however, thanked the doctors and said you have calmed me down. I have no pain. I am fine…

Mom's joy doesn't last long. She has forgotten that she can no longer walk.
- Lower this bed. I want to go to the sitting room! Why have you put me up here?

Shahpur's eyes turn red. He says: Sure mom. Sure.

I lift my brow to signal no! Don't do it!

I call my brother, Kiasha, to come and talk to mom.

Kiasha, her last-born, comes to her bedside and caresses her.
- Mom, you were in a comma. You just came to yesterday and…

And he explains the entire story to mum
- So, I'm at the end of the line.

***

The lady who lives on the fourth floor comes.
- I haven't seen your lady mother for a while now. She always bought fresh herbs and ice cream in the

mornings. She'd say she has bought ice cream for her grandchildren.

I smile. Mom herself liked ice cream and she'd put a few to one side for the grandchildren.

Why do I talk in the past tense!? Mom is still here! Next to me!

- I got worried. I couldn't take it anymore. That's why I decided to come and ask how she was.

I stand at the door. I don't invite her in. I know being seen in her sickbed will cause mom stress. I tell her briefly what has befallen my mother. She leaves and comes back again. This time with salt blessed at Imam Reza's shrine.

- Put some of this salt in the fruit juice and give it to your lady mother to drink. She likes Imam Reza. Imam Reza's God will heal her…

I say I certainly will but abandon the bag on the kitchen table. I jump to my feet though: it might yield results!

I squeeze some fresh orange juice in a hurry and add some of the salt.

Mom has shut her eyes. I say our neighbor came to visit. I spoon-feed her a little bit of the juice. I notice that she swallows it.

I think to myself: Dear God…

Eshagh brings mom fresh flowers every day. He is the firstborn and barely displays his emotions. He arranges the flowers in a vase and puts them next to mom's bed. He kisses her hands and leaves the room tearful. He arranges the rest of the flowers in two other vases and leaves them in the kitchen and sitting room.

The fragrance of the colorful lilia and narcissi fills the house. A breeze blows in through the small gap in the window and flutters the curtain in mom's room.

Mom loves Haydeh. It is Monday, 23 January 2023. From the morning, I had played her the *Jawshan Kabir* prayer performed by Haydeh. I read the Ya-Sin Surah at her bedside from sunrise to sundown. I have fallen short and hang by a thread to find a lifeline.

All the children were there that night. Farshad had made steaks. The voice of Haydeh echoed in the house:

> The world is now a dark place for me
> Life is but a narrow street
> The end of my story is here
> I have been left overweary
> Weary of all humanity
> Weary and tired and lonely
> Oh God, oh God, oh Goood

Mehran massages mom's hands. He swallows the lump in his throat.

- Mehraveh, mom's hands warmed up when I held them in mine.

He presses his lips together further to fight back the tears.

- There was so much I wanted to do for her ... I had such plans ... Why did this happen...

I stroke his arm and say: It will be all right. Don't worry...

And I curse myself for speaking these useless words.

Like mom said, she had only been given a little time from the world above to return to this world and bid farewell to us ... When she had woken up and we were all by her side, she had said this was all she ever wanted: all of us together and happy...

And the following night, she left forever...

I feel choked by sorrow.

You never turned a hair mom. The last curtain of your life was as magnanimous as you were.

You got your wish mom; you left on our shoulders…

Chapter Four

*A man who lives fully is prepared to
die at any time.
- Mark Twain*

Mom was gone. She had said we should be sedate on the day of her burial. Not to cry and sob. Not to wear black. She had said she wanted no ceremony and mosques. She had said to donate all her assets to charity. She had said, just play me a little reed flute...

When she was returned to the earth, we played the reed by her graveside, sang, and honored a life full of love and sacrifice.

Listen to the reed, how it wails
How it laments farewell tales
In the reed, 'tis the fire of love
In the wine, 'tis the ebullition of love

And now, I am left alone in my disbelief. Mom's kith and kin have come for the burial. I tell Fakhri Khanum, why won't mom come into my dreams? She says: She will. Be

patient. Let her find her feet, find her new home. She will come ... And tears stream down her face.

Fakhri Khanum lost her son and husband in car crashes in consecutive years. She says, we lose our loved ones one by one, and one day we will go too…

Freud said the same thing: "Everyone owes nature a death."

My maternal uncle's wife, Pouran, sits next to me. She says: We need our mothers at any age.

My maternal uncles arrive. I hug them. It is as if I'm hugging mom. They feel like mom. How could I have missed that until now? I flutter hither and thither in search of a piece of mom.

The room empties. They also take away the medical equipment. Only a photograph and a pair of glasses are left of mom.

Mom comes into my dream that night. She is feeling good. She is sitting next to me in the car. She says I'm fine. Don't worry about me. I don't need anything at all. Just look after Kiasha…

She had made her promise three times not to be unquiet. She had stretched out her hand to her and said: come here love; promise that you will keep your head high when the day comes…

She was talking about that damned promised day and Kiasha had remained true to her promise. She was overflowing with the force of her sorrow but would not make a sound. She simply looked at me and shed silent tears.

Kiasha is crying out loud. I go to her room.

- I had promised mom but I can't do it anymore.

She is holding something in her hands and kissing it non-stop. I open her hand. It is one of mom's syringes! She had been looking for a candle to light. She had opened a drawer, found the syringe there, and it had set her heart ablaze.

I see Mehran who is watching us. As per habit in his moments of self-restraint, he firmly strokes his beard …

Mina's mom has cooked *abgousht*[1] stew in a stoneware marmite and sent it to us. With fresh herbs and sangak[2] flatbread, vegetables in brine, and pickled beetroot. Mina sets an elegant table. She wants the light to burn in the house. She wants sounds and aromas to sizzle in the kitchen. She says: Mom doesn't like to see you sad. Don't let her spirit suffer.

- Mina, I don't like abgousht.

I get home from school. I go straight into the kitchen as per habit.

"Eww, mom! Why have you made abgousht? You know I don't like it!"

"I've made something else for you. Close your eyes. Don't you dare open them!!!"

I shut my eyes; she puts a bit of food in my mouth, followed by a piece of pickled cauliflower.

"Don't open your eyes. Just enjoy the taste."

"What was it mom? It was delicious!"

---

1. Popular Persian stew made with lamb or beef, chick peas, and beans.
2. Whole wheat flatbread cooked in an oven filled with "little stones" or "sangak" in Persian.

She laughs naughtily and says: "Abgousht love…"

With a morsel of food in her hand, Mina is looking at me frozen on the spot…

I was barely able to sleep that night. Suddenly, I wake up. I feel a calming sensation filling the space above my head. I ask: is that you mom?

It was mom. I'm sure it was her. Her presence filled me with such peace that I fell into a deep slumber like a baby. I dreamt that I was driving with mom sitting next to me; happy and healthy and giving directions!

Turn into this street now … Turn left now…

The address was in Tehran but I didn't know the street.

Next, we reached a T-junction. A road joined the street to the right and left but a wall stood beyond it. Mom kept repeating a name. Something like: *Ram…*

I wasn't sure how to interpret the dream, if it had an interpretation at all, or if it was simply my body's reaction to soothe my ailments and restlessness…

I had this dream three nights in a row in all its details; and at the exact time when we reached the top of the dead-end street, mom wouldn't indicate whether to turn right or left and I'd wake up at once.

I Googled Ram Street but found nothing.

Was mom trying to reveal a secret to me!? Did I have to complete an unfinished task for her? But mom hardly ever left the house and I was pretty much privy to everything in her life! So, what was the meaning of these consecutive dreams?

During the day, I sobbed inconsolably in the house and called out to mom. I hadn't realized that sadness and sorrow are such relentlessly dogged companions.

I am calm for a moment and then a ruthless wave rises and overtakes my entire being. Why is the weight of this endless suffering not alleviated? I can barely breathe. I can hear the sound of my breathing. My heart wants to burst out of my chest. I cannot bear this pain for a moment longer. Why won't it end? It is like the protagonist of a thriller in which the murderer wants to strangle her but she finds the chance to take a few deep breaths and escape her ghastly predicament. I, however, am stuck. I have no escape. The sound of my breathing gets louder. My chest is heaving.

The phone rings. It's Jude. A colleague in Canada. She has no idea I am motherless. I say nothing. She wants to travel with her mother. She wants my advice on which hotel is more suitable to stay in with an elderly mother. She tells me about her mother.

I guide her in one breath. Our conversation ends but not the words lingering in my heart! Hastily, I keep telling myself that I had a mother too ... By God, I also had a mother until a while ago ... I could call her any time I wanted to. She answered my calls straight away. It didn't matter what time of day or night it was. She was always there. Every time I called, her first question was: have you eaten?

The neighbor's wife, the one who brought Imam Reza's

salt, had said the pain never goes away. It will always be with you. She had also lost her parents.

Mom is no longer, and dawn breaks every day. Everyone's back to the grind. It is as if nobody knows what has happened!

Fear. Loss. Loneliness. Going into the kitchen. Cooking with her utensils. Mom's empty place. Nowruz. Chaharshanbeh Suri[1] festivities.

***

Ten days have passed since her passing … I had forgotten those recurring dreams. It is Thursday and I feel impatient and restless. The air does not seem to flow into my lungs. I feel suffocated. I have no choice but to visit her. I listen to her favorite song the length of the way and cry uncontrollably.

As soon as I arrive at her graveside, I kiss her and smell her… All the sounds around me die down at once. I stand, glued to the ground.

I see myself in a misty place … I see my mother and father. They are wearing something similar to Ahram clothing. I can't see their legs. They don't seem to be wearing outfits but they are covered up. They are surrounded by an aura of colorless mist and haze. They are both laughing and telling me that they feel fine. They are in a safe place and do not want to see us grieve.

---

[1]. An ancient Iranian celebration held on the eve of the last Wednesday of the year before Nowruz with bonfires and fireworks.

I am not sure what was it that I saw and what was it that I heard without even speaking; but I felt infinite peace. I open my eyes and hear the hubbub around me again. I shut my eyes and I am by their side again, for a while. I don't know for how many seconds or more, and then there is a whiff of a pleasant fragrance.

I smile. I think, were they truly here with me or did I go to them?

Everything I experience these days is truly pristine; from grief that I never imagined would be so distressing to enchanting spiritual experiences that are both peculiar and believable. I couldn't possibly label them as illusions.

It was January and Tehran was snowy; everything was blanketed in white. The snow kept falling. After the passing of a few hours, I pick myself up from my parents' grave. I sit in the car for a while. I'm not sure where to go. There is no one waiting for me. Nobody wants me to buy them fresh bread, just the one flatbread and no more.

- *Mehi, just the one ... Don't get too many ... Be quick ... I'll be waiting for you...*
- *Sure mom, I'll be there in half an hour.*

Memories come and go relentlessly. Mina had sent a message: Mehraveh, mom always liked to see you strong! Don't let her spirit suffer." And then, she sends me the "Cloudy sky" song by Homayun Shajarian. I know she, too, hasn't been able to hold back the tears.

> The sky is overcast, ask the horizon of my eyes
> These are rain clouds, ask my pouring tears

The weighty waves of sadness will shatter my heart
Ask it of my bosom brimming with gales
Where were you to hear the weeping of my resigned heart...

Homayun's voice reaches its height:

How is it that after you
Sadness sits wherever you were
Where do you sit on this long road,
In this languishing night of farewell,
That through the window of your eyes
I cannot see a glimpse?
In the reserves of my conscience
There is naught but you
Ask the mirror of my soul of what I talk to you
The flames of your love burnt me into ashes.
Ask the ruins of my world
Should you have no faith in me!
How do I endure the sorrow of your love?
Reveal it to me
How do I carry this sorrow to every place?
I cannot depart nor can I stay
How do I reach out to you with my heart?

In the snowfall. Aimless. Purposeless. Hopeless. I just drive...

The snowfall turns heavy.

I notice something and slam on the brakes. The car does

not skid. My legs are shaking. There are no cars behind me. I drive a little forward. How can I believe this…? It's the same street of my dreams over three consecutive nights. I can even remember the shops. I drive on and reach the end of the street, the spot where I always wake up. I turn right and then left, but detect nothing.

What is this place and what is my mother trying to tell me? I turn back to the same spot in my dream, park the car, and get out. I freeze on the spot as I get out of the car. I see the sign of a clinic:

Ram Radiology and Ultrasound Clinic

What am I supposed to find in this building? Is mom trying to tell me she'd still be alive if I had brought her here … Or should I go inside and help someone? Thoughts flash through my mind. It was nearly six in the afternoon. I search Google. The clinic was closed for the February 11th [1] celebrations and would reopen on Sunday[2]. I make an online appointment for Sunday morning.

Perhaps the message mom was trying to send me was inside the clinic. I go home. I sit in front of her photograph and ask her to help me carry out her wish.

Two days pass and Sunday morning arrives. The weather in the capital is still snowy. Once again, I park the car in the same spot where I kept waking up in my dreams. I go inside. Reception guides me to the radiology and ultrasound section. I keep my eyes peeled but only peep at the spaces I can't stare into too inquisitively. I think to

---

1. Anniversary of the Islamic Revolution
2. The working week in Iran begins on a Saturday.

myself: *mom, please help me understand what you're trying to tell me…*

The address and telephone number of a center helping children with special needs are on a noticeboard hanging on the wall. I take a picture of the contact details. I think this must be it. The young girl in admissions asks: have you had an ultrasound before? Do you have medical records here?

I say: no, it's my first time.

She asks: what tests would you like to have?

I say: I'm not sure! Whatever you see fit, given your experience…

Surprised, she glances at me and starts to type. She gives me the bill to pay. I thank her, make the payment, and wait for my turn to go in. Perhaps I'll find something out in there.

The young girl was still scrutinizing me. When our eyes cross, she asks me: Excuse me, but you are different. A lot of people come here every day but your behavior is so different! You seem to be surrounded by a special energy.

And without waiting for my response, she continues: I'm not sure. Maybe you don't live in Iran. Why didn't you go for tests where you live?

She seems like a kind girl. I smile and say, yes love. I don't live here. And unwittingly, I start recounting my dreams for her. I tell her that I have recently lost my mother, and I choke again. I notice that tears well up in her eyes and those of her colleagues. They say they have never heard anything like it. The young girl continues: Maybe this is the energy I saw in you… I smile. I am at a loss for words. I think to myself again: *help me mom*.

It is my turn. I go inside the room. It is half-lit. The doctor asks me a few questions and says that her colleague has told her my story.

I say: maybe I'm delusional ... I don't know, but the only thing that calms me down is to carry out my mother's wishes.

The doctor smiles and says: I'm glad that our clinic is advertised in the other world too! And she begins performing the ultrasound procedure ... At that moment, I see my mother looking at me from above the partition screen and smiling. I seem to have come to the right place. I look at her. My connection with the world is severed every time she comes. The doctor says, I asked if you have a family history of cancer apart from your mother?

- Yes, my father and grandfather...
- I'm very sorry. There are two tumors in your right and left breasts and in your uterus...

She tells me the names of the tumors, which ones are malignant and which ones aren't yet, and that I must waste no time in going to my gynecologist for more tests.

- These must be examined in more detail. You must start treatment and prevention of disease progression...

I can't hear her anymore. I see mom above the white partition of the ultrasound room. She is smiling.

She wanted to make me aware of my disease.

I am not sure why I feel happy. I tell myself that it's all over. I will also leave this life. I didn't want to be here anymore ... I dress up and come out.

The young girl who was waiting for me asked straight away: what happened? Did you find anything out?

I smile and say: everything's fine…
- Thank God for that. Please let me know too if you find out what the message was. You have the number for the clinic, don't you? I'll be here…
- Sure, I will.

And I rush to the car. I need to be alone. What is happening? One after the other…

I get home. I kiss mom's picture that I have placed on the mantelpiece, as well as her spectacles in front of it. I light the candles. It has stopped snowing but the roads are covered in white. I brew some tea and sit next to mom's picture.

Her voice echoes in my head: *Mehi, I've brewed some chai … Bring an estekan if you want some…*

I stare at her picture and ask: mom, was this the interpretation of my dreams? Is this what you wanted me to know?

She smiles. The flames of the candles intensify.

I was silent and still. I didn't feel like doing anything nor did I intend to speak about any of this to anyone. I wanted it to end naturally, while nothing was natural!

It is eleven o'clock at night. The sound of an accordion playing is heard from the street. A traveling musician is playing the "Sultan of hearts"[1] under our window in the middle of a cold wintery night. I put on my coat and go to the front door. I tip him. Thank him. He plays a little more and disappears completely. I think I'm losing my mind.

---

1. Popular Persian song

My mom always cooke a special Azari *alumosama* chicken and prune dish for Chaharshanbeh Suri. She makes the preparations a few days beforehand. Mehran loves mom's aloumosama. Mom always goes the distance. It's a labor of love. She is so filled with life. She *is* love.

She says I don't like frozen foods. My dearest darlings eat this food. Everything must be fresh.

Mehi! This dish needs lots of onions to be tasty ... I tell myself, sure mom ... and I chop the onions. It is Mehran's birthday. It is Chaharshanbeh Suri, mom is gone forever, and I am making aloumosama.

Everyone is here. Norouz is around the corner. Helia has permed her hair. Mina has made a flan dessert. Helia lights the candles on the cake. Mehran blows them out. We hug him. The siblings laugh. They recall memories.

Farshad turns to me and says: this is what mom would have wanted...

Chapter Five

*But in the end, everyone needs more
courage to live than to kill himself.*
- Albert Camus, A Happy Death

The airport taxi is waiting outside the door.
All the lights are turned off.

I look at the window of the house. Mom waves goodbye. She sends flying kisses. It's the middle of the night and she has picked the petals off a rose and put them in a white, flowered porcelain bowl of water. I get into the taxi. She throws the water on the ground after me.
- Ring me when you get there. I won't sleep. I'll wait for your call. I entrust you into God's hands…

She waits at the window for the taxi to turn the corner.

Not once had I ever traveled without a send off. She always got up before me.

Mom had held the Koran for me to pass under even when she was very sick.

The airport taxi is waiting outside the door. I look at the window.

Darkness. Being motherless…

The plane takes off for the UAE. It is a few days before the Norouz New Year. I had traveled with her last spring. On the way there, memories assail me like the painful strokes of a lash. I am doomed to suffer after her. My headphones are on and Mohsen Chavoshi has turned my heart into a graveyard with his song "The springless year"…

The memory of your laughter, mom, has turned into my slayer.

In the book *For a Cup of Coffee in London*, I wrote:

Some people are very noisy, especially when they like something … I won't change the women's laughter for the world. When women laugh … when my mother laughs … I feel everything is fine, everything is calm and peace reigns in the universe … Words fail to describe this calming sensation that I feel.

And now, you have crashed the weight of your sorrow on me, mother, and made my year springless…

I get home. I abandon the suitcase to one side. So what if the Persian Gulf sparkled under the bright sunshine? All the sorrows line up in my heart. I draw the curtains and take refuge in my bed. I am burning up with a fever. I have the chills.

My mobile rings. It's my fiancé. I haven't been able to answer his calls since the day mom left us. I don't wish to burden him with the weight of my loss. He texts me.

"Sweetheart, I am always by your side. You are experiencing a big grief. May God give you patience…"

Adam lives in New York. He is a professor at Long Island University. Parvaneh, our mutual friend who is the chief technology officer of Qatar Airways, has introduced us.

Mom liked Adam. My father was against our marriage. He said it won't have a happy ending. You are not from the same culture. I remember that day very well. Mom was talking to father about Adam's good points and seemed to have persuaded him. After listening to what mom had to say, father got up and went to his room. He returned after a few minutes, uttering a clear: No! I am not happy. It's up to you. I won't attend any of the ceremonies!

Adam applied for an Iranian visa several times but it was rejected because of his American nationality. He finally managed to get a visa after two years and come to visit my family. One of the conditions for an American to obtain a visa was for them to be accompanied by a representative of the Iranian government at all times during their stay in the country. Nevertheless, my father refused to meet him and Adam left Iran.

Nothing went according to plan and I was at the end of my tether trying to cope with a long-distance relationship. I decided to wrap up the previous chapters of my life and move to Canada for my further studies. Although I had closed all communication lines, Adam continued to be in my heart.

My father passed away one year after my immigration. He came into my dream a few nights after his passing. I saw him sitting on top of a tree. He had a very beautiful purple dress in his hand. The length of the dress equaled the length of the tree he was sitting on. He gave me the dress and in a persuaded, joyful tone of voice, he told me: wear this dress when you are with Adam.

I woke up. There was no more Adam; it was over between us.

Falling in love and staying in love needs courage. Love is a self-inflicted pain; a pain that makes your heart grow; a sweet pain you long for with all your being. You seek it out. You let go. You cope with the loss and put in your heart and soul but you come back for more. Nevertheless, I didn't have the courage to suffer again and a few years passed without Adam.

I remember telling my classmate from Tunisia who had recently given birth to her second child: I can't even begin to imagine being a mother. I can't deal with loss. The children stay with you for just a short time and then they fly the nest, shattering your heart into a thousand pieces. And she had said, you can't deny yourself so many years of love just so you won't suffer loss some day! A person without love is like the walking dead! Don't deprive yourself of love! At the very least, you'll see that you are still human, not a robot!

Gibran Khalil Gibran says, "Ever has it been that love does not know its own depth until the hour of separation!"

A few years later, Adam sees Kiana in one of her television programs in London and contacts her, asking about me. And Kiana tells him, she is fine! She lives in Toronto now but she has put her house up for sale and wants to buy a farm and live in nature! It's Mehraveh! She is simply unpredictable!

And Adam asks my sister for my phone number.

It is almost sundown when I see his message. He has written: Mehi, I never doubted my true love for you! Please come back to me. If you marry me, I'll buy you the most beautiful house anywhere you like and hold your hand for as long as you want me!

When I see him again after so many years, he sais Mehi, my life has been blessed, but all of it is nothing without you. I don't love anyone as much as I love you. I will do anything to make you happy. Give me your hand and I will hold it for as long as you are happy with me. You will have my love and support for the rest of our lives.

At last, we were back together and we decided to become engaged last year.

***

Adam texts me again. He is the one I write to but, deep inside, mom is the one I am talking to.

"I feel guilty, Adam. I feel as if I have left mom alone.

She is alone and defenseless on this journey. If only I could be with her ... If only I could take care of her..."

And he replies, you must accept that mommy is gone darling ... You must celebrate that a woman like her has lived and the family she has brought up. You must celebrate her life, Mehi!

***

I am seriously sick. I'm not sure if it is the weight of the sorrow or the cancerous tumors but I don't care. I have lost the will to live.

It is my birthday and Norouz. All the messages I receive begin or end with these two words: *Kind, strong girl*!

Did I seem strong to everyone else!? The tear in the corner of my eye evaporates with the heat of my fever.

I can feel her. She's back. I know it is her. Every time mom comes, I calm down. I see her nodding her head in approval.

I say: Come into my dream mom. Put your hand on my shoulder and squeeze my arm so that I can believe you are here. So that I can believe everything doesn't end after death. So that I can believe you see me. So that I can believe what I'm experiencing are not illusions ... Tell me that you don't want me to come to you yet ... That it's not what you want me to do...

And mom came ... with the same tranquility. She came into my dream, looked at me, hugged me, and squeezed my arms.

In my dream, I yell ... mom ... mom. She smiles and leaves.

The sound of the podcast echoes in the house. The guest of the program is talking about trief and bereavement. About the shock, denial, and not believing that death has happened; anger about our loved one not being there anymore. Regret. Remorse. Depression. Grief. And finally, accepting the reality of death.

Each one of us has also fallen prey to the monster of grief and ignoring it. Kiasha had spent the New Year hour at mom's graveside, planting rosemary and cyclamens for her. She says mom likes the fragrance of rosemary ... The cyclamens sleep at night and their petals open up again with the rising sun.

Seeing them will lift mom's spirit...

Afshar said that he had gone to mom's house, opened the door, and closed it again. He had stood there, key in hand and bewildered. He had said, I'm homeless.

Kiana wrote to me: Can you go and cover mom with a blanket ... I keep thinking she's cold...

Mehran had held my hand and stressed that we must all return to the routine of life! "It will make mom happy, okay? Promise! Okay? Promise ... Promise!"
And then, he had been so restless that he'd gone to visit mom's grave in the early hours of the morning instead of going to work...

Grief was larger than us.

I'm plunged into a deep depression. All the doors have closed on me. Missing mom. Worrying about work. Cancer. My falling weight, and my immune system getting weaker by the day. I had lost everything at once. Total desperation.

I spend every living moment thinking about death in all its detail. I don't want life. I have nothing left. I have experienced all the paths and don't have the courage to live anymore. Nothing brightens my days. There is no hope. I have no incentive. Day and night are the same to me.

Dr. Neda says all of us break in some way following a loss. What is important is how we get back on our feet and put the pieces back together again. Sometimes, we need to go through a long, hard period in search of meaning or ask for help. But if we look for it, we will find it. We may even find meaning in the meaninglessness of life.

I get out of bed. I see the full moon in the sky in the middle of the night. I reach out to it in total supplication and despair. Tearfully, I say: *I am lost…*

At once, all the sounds in my head die down…

Write…

I sense it in my heart. I hear no sound. I am not afraid. I am not even surprised.

Once again, a voice echoes inside me:

Trust your talent…

I can't open my eyes. I experience a peculiar stillness after such a long time. There is a God … There still is a God and he is talking to me … The floodgates open and blur my vision.

The voice carries on:

You must use your creativity to control your life so that you are able to follow your calling. Trust your intuition. You have been given all the knowledge you require in advance. It is time to move forward.

Swiftly, I am overwhelmed by doubt. Am I delusional!?
At that moment, the number appears: 1414.

A positive change in life will present you with the opportunity to heal.

Stop worrying and focus on your inner self.

I have no control over my fingers. They seem to move over the laptop keyboard of their own free will. My mind becomes void of judgment and blame. I carry on typing:

God has a plan for us. Keep calm and allow your inner self to imagine what may even seem impossible to you. Trust and believe that what you long for will come to you. No one will divulge this secret to you. Even if they wish to do so, it will happen in a way that is not comprehensible to you. You will only understand the secret when you are entirely ready. Turn off the extra noises in your head. Sit in a corner and close your eyes. Ask your inner guide to show you the way…

Inadvertently, I pick up the phone to call mom and tell

her what I have experienced in the moment. Straight away, I feel like someone has shot into my heart. I remember that she is no longer here…

I have a shooting pain in my heart. I recall her memories and I miss her even more. Chagrin takes me to pieces.

I get up and write on the whiteboard next to my desk with a green marker:

Show me the way! Give me refuge! And I close my eyes.

You still have a long way to go to complete your life's mission. This is not where it all ends…

Tears well up in my eyes. I see absolute companionship and support around me in great detail.

My inner voice wants me to repeat:

I have faith…

I believe…

I know…

I repeat and tears keep rolling down my face. I see mom smiling … I am calm. Everything calms down when she comes. Never in my life have I had such an experience.

So, God exists. God exists…

The voice continues:

Start writing. You will find the way; you will find yourself … You are unwell because you have lost yourself … Your emotions are the key to your path … It is inside you…

Everywhere is full of light.

Your angels will protect you. Turn off the voices in your head to hear Our voice. Trust the abilities given to you and get up...

Unwittingly, I get up. I search Google and the name "Harper Collins" comes up. I save a picture of its head office in New York and its logo.

I'm not sure why I see the color orange everywhere. Like the desert sand. The yoga mat and the mobile and laptop backgrounds are orange too ... Like sunburned sand!

I spend the entire night meditating and worshipping. I struggle and turn off the intruding voices in my mind to remain a mere observer.

***

I leave the house in the early morning for a stroll.

I desperately need some coffee. On my stroll, I arrive at the same coffee bar where we had tea with mom for the last time. I want to move on but I am so thirsty.

With a lump in my throat, I sit on the same chair where mom sat that night. It was the only empty seat. With a heavy heart, I order some coffee and ask God to look after mom; and if there is a lapse, to admonish me instead of her. My crystal clear mom...

Tears stream down my face.

My coffee arrives.

A young Indian couple is sitting opposite me, arguing.

I want to approach them and say be kind to each other;

you never know what may happen next. Death doesn't warn!

But I would have invaded their privacy! In my heart of hearts, I ask God:

Dear God, sow the seeds of kindness in their hearts...

Just then, the man gives in and takes the woman's hands. He wipes off her tears and she bites into her sandwich!

I was taken aback! My wish had come true on the spot!

I'd like to go to the couple and tell them what just happened.

I don't and I am filled to the brim with a profound joy.

A voice in my head says:

God is our witness ... We are not alone ... We have guardian angels...

God was there. I keep whispering nonstop: Thank you God ... Thank you God ... I keep repeating: Thanks ... Thanks ... lest he should go and abandon me. He must stay for me to last. I had promised to finish the book and then let go of the earth and leave.

***

Adam has said he'll come and we'll go to Cyprus. Adam says we must go to a place where you have no memories of mommy to help you heal. He says I have booked a hotel next to the vineyard you like so much.

We have a stop in Türkiye. I was supposed to land half

an hour earlier than Adam and wait for him at Istanbul Airport for our connecting flight to Cyprus. Suddenly, I have a nervous attack at the airport.

I start sobbing and I can barely breathe. We miss the Cyprus flight and stay in Istanbul.

Love is a healer. His support thaws my frozen spirit. He asks, why have you lost so much weight? I tell him about the tests in brief, not in detail.

He doesn't want to persuade me to get treatment or anything else! No one can persuade me of anything but myself. First, I have to figure myself out in the world.

Adam says I don't believe you are sick; it's mental pressures…

You must look after your diet darling. Then, with a kind

smile, he says you have a gray hair Mehi! Keep it for me. And then he shows me a video clip of the farm.

Adam has built a beautiful house in the heart of a vast farm, next to a roaring river. It has olive and fig trees, various fruit orchards, and a vineyard next to the house. Adam loves cooking. He is skilled in baking Italian and French breads. He has bought a wood-burning stove and is waiting for us to go to the farm so that he can initiate it by baking a pizza margarita. He claims that no one can bake a margarita, and sourdough and focaccia breads, as well as he can, not even Italians! He has asked me to order a dining table made of walnut wood from the forests of Iran. He says wherever we travel, we should get the seeds of that land and cultivate various vegetables in the farm. Adam loves life.

We had planned to start our life together in the New Year but the loss of mom and my loss of myself have postponed the plans.

Adam says, your restless spirit will calm down one day

my darling and I will wait until then.

I couldn't tell him it was not just about losing mom; I had lost all meaning! I don't tell him I have lost absolutely everything! I am crushed. I don't even know what to do with my hands! I don't know what I want to do with life! I have lost everything I identified with; and now, there was no identity or meaning left…

Albert Camus said, "The realization that life is absurd cannot be an end, but only a beginning."

I think there seems to be no escape. Every spirit that enters the corporeal body must reach absurdity to rise again. And it will rise in the end…

I seem to have a lost one in my heart. My eyes keep darting around to find them. How difficult it is to lose … Remember mom, when you cleaned the lentils for your votive offerings, you listened to the poems of Shahriar and murmured: *I am old, and at times my heart remembers my youth…*

Let me turn around you mom. How did I manage to lose you? Proust! O, Marcel Proust, you were so right to say that time is not wasted but lost. Where did the taste of that madeleine cake take you? And these memories are now killing me little by little! What did you go through Proust? Marcel, your day started by dunking madeleine cakes in your morning tea like most French people. You probably closed your eyes when you smelled and tasted the petite madeleine, and that's when the miracle happened and you ascended. And now, this is my life, Marcel! It is not the taste of the madeleine cake but the poems of Shahriar that have made me wretched, Marcel!

I tell Adam that I want to go to Bali. I may take part in the yoga retreats in Bali. After a few days, Adam returns to New York and I book my flight to Indonesia.

Nature. Silence. Seclusion.

The Indonesian driver goes past a beautiful, majestic, and derelict hotel and explains that it has been closed for twenty-five years; it has legal issues. Everyone knows this place as the ghost hotel.

He pauses a little before continuing, we are even afraid of approaching this hotel ... My country has four social stratifications: Brahma, in whom we believe and he is supreme, the rulers and businessmen who own the power and wealth, followed by the army, and then the craftsmen, stockbreeders, and workers, who are in the lowest stratification. I belong to the workers' group.

He explains this without any discomfort. As if he has no quarrels with fate. As if he has made that choice of his own free will.

He stops outside the famous coconut ice cream shop. The display cabinet is filled with young coconuts still in their fresh, green outer skins. The ice cream is served with coconut milk inside the coconut fruit.

I ask the driver to stop along the way at the house where the Julia Roberts movie "Eat, Pray, Love" was turned. The house has been booked for the next six months. I get out of the car. I walk along the narrow path next to the river and find the house! This is it! I am so excited! There is a green plaque on the house on which is written in a pretty, golden font:

EAT
PRAY
LOVE

I walk around a bit. I take a few pictures and recall watching the movie. The places one ends up in! I walk back to the car.

The driver says the film encouraged me to learn English. I hated school, and especially the language classes. When the teacher walked in through one door, I left through the other.

I ask: have you seen the movie?

He laughs and says: "No! I haven't. I didn't even know the address of this house. The movie attracted lots of tourists to our city and I had to learn English. The movie changed our lives."

The Handara Hotel gates are known as the Gate of Heaven. A group of tourists are taking pictures inside the gates. A young girl with golden hair has positioned herself on the ground as a lotus flower and is telling her friend which angle to photograph her from. We walk through the Gate of Heaven.

Hotel Hanadara is vast and beautiful, especially suited to golfers. Some people are playing and a few others are looking after the golf course. I think, are we the ones who decide where in this life we stand? How satisfied are we to choose or not to choose?

I am sitting facing the golf course. A gentle breeze caresses my skin. I am immersed in the beautiful nature. Buddha said if you wish to know God, feel the wind on your face and the warmth of the sun on your hands.

The most important thing that happened is that I understood God exists. Not that I believed, no! Now, I know that He is there. He is the source of light. He is light. Even speaking this absolute truth out loud makes my face feel rosy and warm. I sense Him. I live with Him these days. I calm down when I realize that I haven't been abandoned. I know it is not an illusion. Like watching the clouds and the shapes they form in the sky, all of which speak to me. Like the life force in the trees. Like the soothing scent of the Persian rose. The fragrance of flowers is neither an illusion nor does it need signs and proof. I feel good with the scent of the rose; with the wobbly dewdrops on the pink petals that wobble my heart too, with zest.

I think how unaware I am of this labyrinthine life, only ensorcelled by my childish games and successes! I never dreamt that experiencing these intuitions and discovering these revelations would be so attractive to me. I am put to shame for having a superficial view of this magnificent universe. What a good decision it was to come to Him!

I sit and look at the majestic nature. Something sinks in my heart. The universe embraces me. All the crying, tears, loneliness, falls, losses, miseries, end of lines, and this feeling of nihilism and futility … My trajectory throughout these years has not been an easy one by any stretch of the imagination and still isn't. I believe that overcoming the distractions and facing the fear of suffering means that life wants to slowly show a different side to me. I laugh. I think it was all worth it…

I watch the people. Hard at work but happy and nimble. One is making handicrafts outside his home. He has dug and brought exquisite rocks from the heart of the mountain and says that they are healing. He says, I have carved a health mantra on them. He puts a colorful stone bracelet on my hand and recommends another purple one which will look good next to the colorful palette. I take both. Not for his sales skills but for his soothing tone and enthusiasm when he speaks of making his artwork. I think that perhaps the inhabitants of big, progressive cities experience more suffering and depression compared to simpler societies.

After the 1979 Revolution, Iranians were scattered around the world like rosary beads. In the middle of a mountain forest in Ubud, a group of loud and lively African tourists with braided hair laugh from the bottom of their hearts. They are sitting at the next table and are making a video call. They say it's Pani joun's[1] birthday! They synchronize to say, "Happy Birthday Pani joun" in

---
1. Dear - A term of endearment in Persian

unison. One of them asks, is her name Pani Joun? One of the girls explains: No! In Persian, people call those they like "joun". And they joyfully speak to Pani.

I have entrusted myself to the universe. I sit on the terrace at the hotel. At the heart of the mountain forest. It is raining. I have a big smile on my face! Bali transforms everyone. The rain intensifies. I cry and I laugh. I've turned into quite a Mona Lisa! I get drenched in the rain. Everyone takes cover under the awnings. I want to resist. I want to see the rainbow. Every decision has its pros and cons. It is the law of nature and I don't want to fight nature. I want to understand it and become one with it.

I am at the heart of the Indonesian forest and its beauty has mesmerized me.

Its wild, quirky rainfall is making me whimsical!

I'm beginning to get it into my head to stay here, not to return.

I see several large lizards on the wall.

In the hotel guidebook, under the picture of insects and reptiles, it is written:

Dear guests, do not be afraid! These are harmless.

I think the consequences of decisions can at times be harmless but not every guest can bear it. I decide to focus my mind. Make it sharp and cutting, like a laser beam. Attention is the most vital ability of humans and everyone is trying to steal it. I, too, am doomed to suffer the modern disorder of ADHD, of the adult kind of course!

In the rain, I decide to focus my body, mind, thought, and energy, to see the flames of fire and warm up, when, just then, I see the word "rescue" before my eyes. I seem to be standing in the safest place of my life. A voice in my head says:

Can't you see that light is fighting for you! It takes your hand and you ignore it! The light holds on to your hands. Do not doubt the good events. Open up your arms…

I come to myself at once. I see that a big smile is on my face and I am totally drenched. Was it nature that did all this?

I wake up in the early morning hours with the sounds of nature. I step on the cobble stones dug out of the mountains that decorate the hotel bathroom. I draw a few deep breaths. I bow to the mountain forest. I say hello to the sun and gulp down all the clear forest air. I turn on the hot water. I imagine that light is showering on my head and face. I shut my eyes. I am submerged in light. The sound of birds chirping is heard from the heart of the mountain opposite. I lift my hands and allow the water, this miracle worker, to slip from the tip of my fingers and wash away all my pain and suffering. The sounds of nature polish my spirit…

I make coffee and go on the balcony. I open the laptop and search on Google. I have decided to get my first Tibetan bowl from Ubud. I find the "Temple of Sacred

Sounds". Google says that it is a hike of an hour and a half to the temple. I set out. The weather is fantastic. I have lost myself to all this beauty. I cross at the heart of the forest. There is only me, the towering coconut trees reaching out to the sky, rice paddies, the beckoning sounds of nature, and the wild tropical showers that pour at times, only briefly. The sun is showing from underneath the clouds. I deliver myself into the light. Unwittingly, I tell myself I am of light. I entrust myself to the source. I will not stray far from the nucleus. And I am immersed in light at once. This energy is undeniable. I feel propagated by light. I become the light. I walk and I meditate. I think the best and most beautiful blessings in the universe can neither be seen nor heard. They must be sensed by the heart.

I have been walking for an hour when I am engulfed by fear…

You've come alone to the forest! With no tools! What if there is an intruder!? What if an animal attacks you!?

I have selected my thoughts. I have chosen fear. At that moment, several black dogs appear and bark at me. Fear is a reaction but courage is a choice. I don't run away; I gather myself quickly. I turn off my fear and choose courage. I bend down slightly and pretend to pick up a stone. The dogs leave.

I continue on my path. A stone staircase appears in front of me. I climb down. I cross a wooden bridge over a roaring river and arrive at a temple in the heart of the forest.

A spring bubbles up underneath the temple. I see a woman fill a large glass jar from the water source. She places it on her head and climbs up the stairs.

At a later date, I conducted a search and found that the Pura Tirta Tawar is a sacred water source and the people of Bali believe that anyone who drinks from it will live over a hundred years.

Finally, I arrive at my destination two hours later. A white and a black dog run towards me, barking to inform their owner that a stranger has entered their territory!

I ask the landlady, do you know where the shop of "Sacred Sounds" is? And immediately add the shop of Tibetan bowls before she has a chance to be taken aback by my question!

Contrary to my expectations, the woman is not surprised at all. She says: it's right here! In my house! Upstairs. But you must make an appointment!

"I had no idea! I have come through the forest on foot to get here."

There is a green wooden sign opposite the woman's house, saying: Yoga Retreat.

"It is now time for my prayers. I must be present every sundown at six o'clock. I have never missed a day. You can come inside and wait for me to finish my worship."

"Yes, of course!"

Her house has a high level of energy. She says you can sound the bowls. It won't distract me.

One of her dogs comes along and stares into my eyes. Then, she lies on the sofa. She keeps an eye on me now and then. I take the mallet and gently tap it around the rims of the bowls. I listen to the sounds of the singing bowls.

A woman has set up a temple for herself in a corner of her house facing a window from the panes of which coconut trees can be seen. In a low voice that I cannot hear, or more accurately that I have no comprehension of, she murmurs some words. Her voice takes on a singing tone as if she is repeating a mantra. She lights a few sticks of wood. Her voice mingles with the sounds of the Tibetan singing bowls as she worships. My mind relaxes. The room is filled with handmade Tibetan bowls and large, colorful, crystal bowls. I play with the sounds. Their echo seems to balance my busy mind. I think the dog trusts me now and her mind is put at rest. She no longer eyes me, or perhaps the echo of these sounds has turned her mind off too.

Diane finishes her worship and comes. I have figured out her name from the name of the shop, "Sacred Sounds with Diane".

She puts a yoga mat on the floor. She addresses me: ask your heart which bowl is yours! Pick three bowls according to your intuition.

I pick three bowls and sit on the mat. Gracefully, she shows me how to make the bowls sing. I close my eyes. The vibrations of the Tibetan bowls reverberate in my being. Now, I know which one is mine.

As I listen to the sounds with my eyes shut, she asks, what message does the sound send you?

I can't help but say: *you are not alone* ... and I hug my bowl.

I don't feel my feet on the ground. I seem to be on the clouds...

***

The balcony of my room in the Conrad Hotel overlooks a stunning mountain over which magnificent trees have grown. Ubud's tropical weather turns everything lush and gives it life, even the hard rocks. My suite is on the fifth floor. However, since the hotel has been constructed on a mountain, the balcony is at the same level as the mountain forest that is my view. The sound of the Sungai Petani river roaring between the hotel and the mountain echoes in the dead of night.

I sit on the balcony for a while and listen to the sound of the river. I have to leave beautiful Ubud tomorrow and return to Toronto to put my affairs in order.

I miss mom. I think a relationship is different from love. You are always the conqueror in love even if you are vanquished but you must be the winner in a relationship. The days in love are but a short interval to give love and kindness; it's a time to tell yourself if only I had done the other thing for them too, even after you have lost them. You are not self-righteous in love. You don't hold anyone to ransom in love. You simply regret not spending more time with the other person. Why didn't I make them happier? Why didn't I buy those figs on the day she wanted them and said there's no time now? Leave it for later! Damn all the days that I lost in confusion. Why did I get stuck in Canada and work on the files at a time when the whole world was affected by COVID! Mom called every day and said she missed me ... And I woke up one day and realized that I had lost the sunshine of my life ... Now, I will give everything just so I can call her; just for a second!

What does it matter how hard I had tried to complete everything and get excellent results. That day had arrived and I was faced with something I never dreamt of. So unexpected! I could gain more money and success but couldn't buy more time. Never! And life had a snowball's chance in hell, melting away under the hot sun and ending...

My chest hurt badly yesterday. I was even briefly unable to breathe. I didn't want to be surprised again. What am I doing to this life? Why have I trapped myself in this global race? Where am I trying to go? Why won't I break these chains? Who am I? Why am I here? I had watched mom go with my own two eyes, without taking anything with her.

That's that. The final whistle!

I shut the door on my thoughts and the balcony at the same time and take refuge in sleep. I wake up in the middle of the night. A spectrum of colors from the heart of the mountain forest opposite the room is shining through the glass and wood door of the balcony into the room.

It's a spectrum of beautiful, colorful lights the likes of which I have never seen in my life. The ceiling is full of light; a seamless tranquillity. I'm not surprised. I just watch.

I ask: *is that you mom?*

It was mom. I calm down every time she comes, like a little child.

The light stays afloat on the ceiling for a short while, then twists into a tunnel of spiral colors, and leaves through the window, sinking into the heart of the mountain.

I whisper: thank you mom ... and sink into a deep sleep.

I was not alone. She hadn't left me alone. Mom wasn't the body I had interred. Mom is this beautiful spirit. Mom isn't finished. Mom is boundless. Mom is eternal. Mom is light.

A great spirit always takes care of everyone. A great spirit is immortal. Maya Angelou said it once.

Chapter Six

Remember that everyone you meet is afraid of something, loves something and has lost something.

-*H. Jackson Brown Jr.*

I walk past North York Cemetery. I remember mom. She used to say, *I'd like to come and live with you in Canada at the end of my life and die here. The cemeteries here are so serene...*

Mom did not want to die. Who would look for a serene cemetery to die that mom should look for one! She loved life. How could anyone who had experienced so much hardship and chagrin still love life ... I see the clock. It displays the time as 1515: *trust the universe...*

My guardian angel wants me to believe in its guidance and support.

Following intuitions requires courage. I draw a deep breath and wait for more signs. For the first time in my life, I don't want to follow logic and reason. I have shut the door on reasoning. Point final!

Intuition acts as a protective light for me. I understand

it; it's not far from me and it's not a stranger to me. It has always been there. I had disregarded it! I don't need details like where the codes have come from and who has written interpretations on them. I feel at ease; I have not been abandoned to my own devices. I am connected to the source. I watch the sky; an expanse I hadn't lifted my head to watch in a long time. I had forgotten it and only saw the skyscrapers.

As Arthur Schopenhauer said, we are all caught up in a hopeless cycle of wanting things, getting them, and then wanting more things. When mom passed, it taught me that we don't own anything or anyone in this world. My only asset and fallback is my experience and the lessons I've learned. There is no certainty and conclusiveness and everything is fleeting. Life is also fleeting. Humans seek more money to satisfy their power mongering and illusions, and eventually end up in a theatrical life. They create an identity out of their supposed triumphs and are immersed in gratification while always fearing that their false identity may become damaged and collapse.

I keep repeating to myself that you don't own anything in this world! I have suffered the pain of dependence. I must not be trapped by it again. The pain of dependence and then loss ... Dependence is at the root of all suffering. I have seen with my own two eyes that, like it or not, everything and everyone I'm attached to will leave me one day, or I will inevitably leave them. Dependence creates suffering. Move on Mehi! Don't get stuck in a rut! Your job is to just experience and love! Leave all the creatures in the world alone! Beauty lies in freedom, not bondage! Nothing and no one belongs to you! Accept and move on.

This suffering is a warning sign; it is a sign of spiritual wakefulness. I must face it to awaken and remain alert. According to Camus, when a man has learned how to remain alone with his suffering, then he has little left to learn.

I place my hand on my chest, bow to the sky, and start walking.

I walk into the Japanese restaurant. A middle-aged waitress in a red kimono bows to the guests at the door and welcomes them.

The hands of the wall clock rotate on the sushis and

sashimis. According to sashimi time, it is four in the afternoon. A young girl with emblematic Japanese poise comes forward and says: I remember you. Would like some green tea again?

It was raining outside and the green tea and soup revived me. Oblivious to the world, I was in Japan! Oblivion is so wonderful ... Turning your mind off momentarily and hearing the voice of a beautiful girl at the table next to you saying enthusiastically to the young man sitting opposite her: I love ginger!

The sizzling sound of beef teriyaki ... the smell of crunch noodle soup ... Japanese music...

Why do I choke up? Could it be that the grief suddenly overwhelming me is the same as love, and all the unspent love collects in the corners of my eyes, my throat, and the void in my chest, and I am still alive and witnessing these wonderful moments...

Life is in front of me and I am standing exactly in the middle of life's flow to plunge my face into the purple acacia flowers by the side of the street and be intoxicated; to hear the heartfelt laughter of little girls and impatiently wait for a romantic message; the smell of fresh coffee; the smell of rain on soil; the deep breath of liberation; meditating before sunrise; finishing off a book or a series; and returning home after a long day or trip...

Who knows what will happen next.

The chef comes dressed in red and a white toque. He smiles and starts to eat his own cooking with his assistant.

On the side of my plate, there are a few shiso leaves;

it's the same as our mint or pennyroyal. Mom loved pennyroyal. Whatever she cooked, pennyroyal was there too, from buttermilk *aush* to pennyroyal tea. She always said I brought you up on pennyroyal.

I have had an argument with Adam and I am upset with him for having hung the blue evil-eye beads we bought in Türkiye on the wooden wall next to the house that we were supposed to hang together without waiting for me! I knew I was looking for excuses! But I didn't know what I wanted and what I was fighting for. That is why I didn't pick my fights smartly! I was aimless, or perhaps looking for an excuse to say that all you out there are responsible, and free myself of all the responsibilities I had to shoulder. I send Adam a picture of the seeds I bought yesterday.

He sends a message, when you are in a better mood, buy a sample of every pennyroyal family and bring it with you, darling.

I don't want to leave Japan and enter Canada.

Nevertheless, I am also aware that if I stay too long, I'll start feeling agitated here too. Adam told me once, you must learn to relax. I drink up my green tea and leave Japan. It is still raining. I've never had an umbrella, or maybe I did, I don't know. In any case, I've never used one. I like getting wet in the rain. Once, Adam sent me a picture of Stanley Tucci carrying an umbrella, seemingly at the Tokyo International Film Festival, and wrote: where can we get this umbrella from? He wanted us to get a large umbrella for two for our farm so that the two of us could walk under it in the rain and snow. I didn't tell him I've never walked with an umbrella in the rain. I did a search. Stanley's umbrella was made by Royal Walk Umbrellas in the UK. I ordered them in black, navy blue, and green but not the red meant for ladies. He has received the umbrellas by now. I walk in the rain. I used to call mom around now. As soon as she picked up the phone she'd say, I was thinking about you just now. I've been wanting to call you all morning. I dreamt about you last night. And then, she'd tell me her dream and ask me to interpret it. I only gave good interpretations. I'd say this is good mom. You'll soon get some good news. Grief changes your phonebook and transforms your sorrow into stories. You become a storyteller.

In life, joy lasts for a fleeting moment but grief, sorrow, and pain can at times stay with us for years. Life has no logical basis. Even so, nobody can stay on this earth forever. We must someday leave this baseless life. I think it may be the pleasant experience of death that makes life bearable! Maybe it is valuable because it ends! I see myself in the window of the flower shop. Mom has also taken the sparkle of my eyes with her…

***

I hug mom's outfit and lie down on the bed. Her dress. Her butterflies. Nothing gets back to normal. I feel everything is all right one minute, and then I see that I am broken the next. I don't know this part of myself. I am confused … I am experiencing a painful time … I hadn't understood the meaning of loss and grief until now. I am broken and all my efforts to piece myself back together are in vain.

I hadn't chosen this pain. I think my only option is how to deal with it. Like all the other times that I had to face the pain of loss, failure, or betrayal.

I ask myself, how original has my approach been? How have I coped? Do my character and behavior have the strength to stand up to the absurdity and meaninglessness of life?

My Canadian friend, Steve, had lost his Portuguese wife on their honeymoon in Lisbon. A sudden stroke! Unexpected! Brokenhearted, he had returned to Toronto. I still had mom in those days. I did not perceive this man's grief. To console him, I used to tell him that death is real. And now, I realize that nothing is more painful than when your grief is denied!

He had asked me, do you know a hair transplant clinic in Türkiye? How can I make an appointment and go there for a hair transplant? I had said, is this necessary in your mental state? And with an endless sorrow in his eyes, he had responded that his wife had asked him a few times enthusiastically to have a hair transplant but he had not paid any attention. And now, the regret was driving him crazy...

Nowadays, I understand that experience enriches life and alleviates remorse. Living is nothing but experiencing, and it is this very experience that destroys you! And if you can get back on your feet again, it will remake you as new.

***

Priyanka has messaged me: I've enrolled you on the course. It starts tomorrow.

Priyanka is from India and immigrated to Canada a few years ago. Four years ago, we met at a complementary class for our law course and have remained in touch ever since. A few days ago, she told me that she had just come across "The Art of Living Foundation" and that, for fifty dollars, I can have unlimited access to their classes and support. She said she had been able to find the roots of many of her vulnerabilities by attending just one course and finding profound peace in her life, which she didn't have previously! Her stress and anxiety levels had also dropped and the quality of her life had improved.

The courses are online. The instructor starts the class at five in the morning, India time.

The instructor is a middle-aged woman with short, black curly hair and an agile body. She is wearing an Indian outfit and is sweet-spoken and loveable. I like her from the word go. The participants are from diverse countries. After introducing the class, Sharma poses three questions and gives us fifteen minutes to answer them.

Who or what do you belong to in your life?
What do you need in life?
Why do you think you need it?

I, who always have an answer to every question about myself, am left flabbergasted.

Who do I belong to? I am like a particle suspended in the air. The pain of loss overcame me again. I say, I don't know who or what I belong to but I believe I need peace and happiness to find my way. If only I could take control of my affairs…

Sharma says you belong to us and we belong to you. We are not separate from one another. And she asks the class to embrace me. Everyone opens their arms; it's virtual but I feel the warmth and the floodgates open.

Sharma continues, take a deep breath everyone. Breathing cleanses the body. We must breathe to exist. Breathing is the secret of life. Commit to your breathing: inhale, exhale … inhale, exhale.

Concentrate on your body. You will notice that your breathing pattern changes at times of laughter, anger, fear, and anxiety. It's broken when you are afraid. It stops. Focus on your breathing when you laugh. Breathing is not separate from you for even a moment. Inhale and exhale deeply to relieve your pain and sorrow.

In bygone days, a fire had to be lit at the start of day to boil water. To light the fire, it had to be blown into. The day began with a deep, continuous inhaling and exhaling. Breathe deeply. A major part of our body consists of water and air. Breathe and don't let toxic materials enter your body. We cannot stop breathing. Drink water to keep up energy levels in your body.

Now, breathe in through your mouth. Put your hands on your ears and breathe. Listen to the sounds of the universe.

In Sanskrit, prana means life force. Prana regulates the breathing and helps us to concentrate on the purpose of life.

Eat portions the size of the palm of your hand because that's the size of your stomach. Get enough sleep to get rid of tiredness and no more. Don't stay idle. Carry on with your daily activities and breathe. Breathing is a type of exercise. Focus on your breathing. It's a type of meditation and will build your way of thinking.

Sit with folded knees like the Japanese when you eat. This technique will make you agile and help your balance. You concentrate and keep your balance…

Sharma talked to us for nearly three hours. We meditated and practiced the breathing techniques but didn't feel the time pass. I think all the deep breathing had relaxed my mind.

At the end of class, she says: we will pray for peace, quiet, and love. And we all say: namaste.

We were given assignments for the next three days; not to drink coffee and alcohol; eat vegetarian meals; take ten deep breaths fifteen minutes before sleeping and after waking up; and meditate.

***

I go shopping for the vegetables at a shopping center near where I live. Halfway there, suddenly it starts to pour and I have to take a taxi.

The middle-aged Russian driver speeds his Tesla anxiously and gets impatient at every stop sign. He says we don't have these in Russia. Everyone is so slow here. He says he failed his driving test several times just because he was going too fast! And he keeps repeating he failed me because I was quick! And he adds triumphantly, but I finally got my driver's license.

And I am happy that I have finally reached my destination and can get out of his car.

I had practiced my breathing and meditation that morning but failed my next assignment, which was to refrain from drinking coffee. With the first smell of coffee, I walk into a coffee bar, which is also a flower shop in addition to serving coffee.

The coffee shop was exquisitely decorated with colorful peony flowers. The aroma of coffee and roses filled the space. Tea and coffee were served in pink pots and cups with small sandwiches and scones, in the traditional English cream tea style. A small glass vase was placed on each table, holding a few wildflowers.

I order an almond croissant and coffee. From the corner of my eye, I watch the Ukrainian girl to see when her patience will run out. Calm and collected, she continues to carry out the orders of a middle-aged Chinese lady.

- No, dear girl. Take out the purple flowers and put these small pink ones in that white terracotta vase ... The big one, no! Bring the small one. That doesn't look good! Switch the vases...

She brings me iced coffee. I say I asked for hot coffee. She says I'm distracted. I'll change it straight away.

As soon as I drink the coffee, it gives me a new lease of life. I feel slightly guilty for not listening to Sharma but my sin was delicious. I see the tablecloth and I am thrown back to the day when mom said she wanted a tablecloth for the breakfast table…

I look at tablecloths. They are all beautiful. I am in two minds between two. The young girl standing next to me feels the material and addresses me: it's so difficult to choose! She glances at the two tablecloths I'm holding, narrows her eyes, and says: I think this red, checkered pattern is nice for Christmas. I smile and say, I'll take both.

Mom likes both tablecloths. She says, use the one with the checkered pattern now. And she never used the other one. It was spread over mom's grave and I never saw it again.

I can no longer set foot in any of the shops … How can anyone have such a prominent presence everywhere!

***

I promptly get ready for class every day. Priyanka sends a message. I reassure her that I haven't missed class.

Today, we spend fifteen minutes practicing the Om mantra. At the end of the mantra, Sharma asks us how we feel. One of the participants who has lost her father is restless. Sharma quotes the spiritual leader, Sadhguru, and says: "If you want to humiliate the loved one you have lost, make them the source of your suffering! But if you want to cherish them, make them the source of your happiness in life."

Another one speaks of adultery with hate and anger and that her fiancé ditched her at the altar.

Gently, Sharma says, let your tears roll down. These are toxic. Don't interpret toxicity. Let go. Release it. Accept people as they are. Don't become someone else's football. Forgive yourself and everyone else. You are now here and safe and sound. Live in the moment. You are the one responsible for your emotions, not others. If you blame it on someone or something else, you will be robbed of your happiness. You will be helpless. You will have expectations. We may even change our own views at any given moment. We can barely control our opinions; so, how can we rein in other people's beliefs and what they think about us? If you wish to become a master, focus on your breathing technique. Blame will take you nowhere. Say you won't be sacrificed by your emotions. I am the master of my own mind. I am the master, not my mind! Be in the moment to avoid blaming yourself and the others. Snap your fingers and come into the present. Let go of the past.

Accept trials and tribulations, such as losing loved ones; testing times; we do not wish to be tested but we accept it; like being burgled; nobody wants a thief in their house but it happens! Acceptance is the first lesson. Accept and move on. Joy means being in the moment, like children; like nature.

If life progresses calmly in a normal manner, it will be like a boring movie! Mountains and foothills are more beautiful when they are next to each other. They are alive. Like heartbeat. Look into your inner self; that's where all the answers are. In this way, you will find peace, and peace is complete power.

Energy moves wherever the attention is focused on. Focus on pleasant, positive wishes and sow their seeds in infinite possibilities, bless them, and give thanks for the realization of your new life. Wake up from meditation as if everything has already taken place. Observe the synchronicity and give thanks. If you are in the moment, you will create; in other words, you will allow yourself to enter the infinite realm. Thoughts and words have power. You must carefully see where your thoughts are taking you. Negative thoughts take away your peace. Stress takes away the positive currents from us. Make peace with yourself. Obstacles are a sign that we must wake up. Choose the harder task. Making an effort brings joy. The environment impacts us. You may have to change your group of friends. Find new friends who are aligned with your wishes and goals. Look further afield. See the dream that you know will happen and put your all into it. Don't allow your concentration to be lost on things that steal your focus away. It is only desire that creates the unseen. In this experience, the biggest waste of time is to compare your life to that of others. See what you're afraid of. This will be the starting point for your growth. The clearer your mental image, the more self-confidence you'll have, and you won't lose time. If we find out one day that we have been wrong, that's okay. We will review things and use our experiences to begin with a new image. Great ambitions create great hope.

Once Sharma finished, there was a smile and the light of hope on the girl's face.

Sharma continues by saying, now put a raisin in your mouth, and don't swallow it until I say so. Taste it and savor it with all your being. You will see how you'll understand its taste in more detail! Be one hundred percent present in everything you do. When you eat, eat one hundred percent. When you listen, be all ears one hundred percent. When you talk, talk one hundred percent. Do your one hundred percent in the present moment, like eating this raisin! Don't rush your food. Don't walk too fast. Don't talk too fast. Breathe! This will make you humble; it will calm you.

To be creative at all times, you mustn't allow your body to be on autopilot. Take every step with awareness.

Next, Sharma asks us to close our eyes and imagine that we are a baby who is a few months old. And she describes every second to us, from childhood to old age and finally death.

I close my eyes and review my life from childhood to adulthood. It's like watching a movie ... Even the sufferings and peaks and troughs seem attractive to me. It is like a pulse! Alive and dynamic ... I think to myself, so why did I make it so hard!

At the end of the life cycle meditation, Sharma says that this life is like a dream. Enjoy the game of life. In the end, we are all in the same boat. So why worry!

The first course is completed. Sharma says, now lie down and watch this short video. The video showed the philanthropic activities of the spiritual and humanitarian leader, Gurudev Sri Sri Ravi Shankar, who established "The Art of Living Foundation" to promote a peaceful society and humanitarian values. At the end, we realize that the fifty dollars we have paid were in fact spent on philanthropic projects. Our instructor, Sharma, was also a member and volunteer at the foundation for promoting love and peace.

Sharma asks us to pray for the peace of the person who has brought us into the group. And I pray for my friend, Priyanka…

Mom reconciled me with the skies and this meditation course reconciled me with my inner self. What was I looking for out there? I am just beginning to understand that the answer to all my restlessness and questions is within me.

Mom's leaving transformed the meaning of many things in me. Now, I see the breadth of life in the breadth of death. I understood the real meaning of life when I understood the meaning of death.

I think everything has a finale; it has an ending; there is a finish line and perhaps this is what gives meaning to life, like a book which must have a final chapter.

According to Carl Gustav Jung, people either shun pain and suffering, tend to ignore it, or generally avoid it. But pain is the symbol of growth and progress. It is a warning by the body which is trying to attract attention to that part. Suffering must not make you unhappy. This is where people are often wrong. Suffering is supposed to make you aware of the fact that your life needs to change! People become more aware only when they are wounded. Suffering must not increase desperation. Don't suffer your pain, understand it! This is an opportunity for wakefulness. When you become aware, your desperation ends.

In the last moments of his life, Albert Einstein said: I have done my share. In reply to a priest who said may God bless your soul, Charlie Chaplin said: Why shouldn't he? After all, my soul is His! When taking his last breaths, Victor Hugo said: I see a light. And in his last moments, Goethe had said: More light. George Bernard Shaw had said: Well, it'll be a new experience, anyway.

Beethoven's last words bring a smile to my face. He said: The comedy is over. Before dying, Newton said: I do not know what I may appear to the world, but to myself, I seem to have been only like a boy playing on the seashore and diverting myself in now and then finding a smoother pebble or a prettier shell than ordinary, whilst the great ocean of truth lay all undiscovered before me. Humans have no real assets but themselves and their inner awareness is the only capital they take with them when leaving this planet.

I ask myself, how do you want your story to end?

I watch "The fountain". Hugh Jackman portrays the character of Dr. Tommy Creo who is looking for a cancer cure to save his wife Izzi (Rachel Weisz). Hugh Jackman denies that death exists. When he loses his wife, he says at her graveside: death is a disease and has a cure. I will find it...

Last night, I experienced some strange events when meditating. I seemed to be having a conversation with someone who looked very much like me.

As my meditation became deeper, a vivid and captivating scene unfolded in front of me. I saw a city along a flowing river. Its waters peacefully crashed against some smooth rocks and intertwined, creating a peaceful scene. The landscape evoked a profound emotional reaction in me and left me tearful. In this mental journey, a presence similar to myself inspired a fascinating revelation in me. It did not speak but I understood everything it wanted to say. It said: one day, I will call this city by the river my home…

It was as if this future possibility had been instilled in my consciousness. Amid the revelations, I came face-to-face with mom. She was dressed in white from head to toe. She was healthy. She was peaceful. Her presence gave me reassurance and confirmed my observations. In her peaceful manner, she stated that my spiritual dimension took care of her and she lived in peace. Namely, the same girl who looked like me but was illuminated, had no wounds and seemed to have no pain.

Mom wanted to put my mind at rest. And then, she disappeared.

I wake up. A blue light has filled the entire ceiling. I get a message from my friend, Charlotte. She writes I am in Lisbon, Portugal. I have bought a ticket to Madrid for tomorrow … And she has sent a few pictures taken in Lisbon.

Charlotte hadn't been content and happy lately. She

said I think I have to leave this place. I am caught up in everyday life. I'm not happy here.

It took her a few months to finally decide. She sold her apartment and gifted her household goods to those who needed them. I was with her when she gave the last box of her belongings and clothes to the neighbor's daughter. She said: I feel light, and showed me the route of her journey on the map. Enthusiastically, she said: it starts here. I have a stop in Washington. Then, I'll travel to Italy, France, Portugal, Spain, Egypt, and Türkiye…

I had never seen Charlotte so happy. Perhaps it is right to say that people are not trees to stay in one place and spread their roots. Charlotte left her life in Toronto and went to see the world with a small suitcase and figure out what she wanted out of life…

I write to Charlotte and say that I am meditating. I ask: Charlotte, am I delusional?

"Hello love. I haven't tried this meditation before but I've read several books on it that said the source of these images or sounds is from higher above … I don't think it is an illusion…"

And she sends a picture of Lisbon's popular dessert and my favorite, Pastel de Nata. She writes:

"I tried this custard tart you told me about at the famous Pastéis de Belém café! It was great…"

I think we are all lost. Or perhaps, everything turns topsy-turvy in life and there is a typhoon so that everything can fall into place. I recall Oprah Winfrey's talk show when she said in the aftermath of Hurricane Katrina that when love touches your heart, it leaves a trace so that you will always remember the feeling that someone loved you and that you were important to them.

She said I was leaving Houston one early morning, eight days after the hurricane, when I saw a young father carrying his sleeping six-year-old daughter. I stopped and asked: "Sir, how will you cope with this situation?"

He replied: "I'll cope with it because we have survived this disaster and we will now move with the power of love. And I have never felt so much love in my entire life."

And Oprah had said: "I'm sure that you'll take charge of the situation."

***

We go to the seashore with Priyanka to watch the sunset. In a mischievous tone, she says: Are you watching Charlotte?

I nod and say: yes, I saw her Instagram posts yesterday. By the way, why did she return to Barcelona? Wasn't she supposed to go to Türkiye after Egypt?

Then, we both stare at each other with sparkling eyes for a split second and start a video call with her.

Charlotte answers the phone happily and says laughing out loud: I knew you'd call today! You've guessed right … I've found the love of my life here in Barcelona … Get ready for my wedding…

I think to myself, life is full of surprises but you must make a move to be surprised. When your inner world is raging and won't let you rest, perhaps something is waiting for you further afield…

Chapter Seven

Close your eyes and hold your breath,
everything will be really pretty.
- Steven Spielberg – "Close encounter of the third kind"

According to Jung, "depression is like a woman in black. If she turns up, don't shoo her away. Invite her in, offer her a seat, treat her like a guest, and listen to what she wants to say."

"There is a crack in everything. That's where the light gets in". Pain is a message for an outwardly pause, an inwardly encounter, and discovering revelations that will pave the way for your new identity. This sit-in with your Self will change your narrative of existence.

Dr. Neda's voice echoes in my ear. Embrace pain. Don't evade it. Grief changes your identity; it's like a black mark on your heart; like the black heart of poppies. There is no way out. You must make your heart bigger. The vessel of your being must get larger to endure the chagrin. Loss changes the meaning of life. Experiencing grief and loss changes you into another person. It transforms you. If you haven't changed yet, it means that acceptance has not occurred and you haven't accepted its reality yet. Let go of the chord to let in the new meaning. Life is an experience. We have been given one chance in this lived experience and there are no guarantees that it will be pleasurable. It can be filled with challenges. Grief can be your unlived life. Grief removes all the inner hurdles we have placed on the path of love. After moving on from an unpleasant event, growth can take place. We can be in charge of how we spend our remaining days.

I look at her. Now, mom was no longer there to buy me cream cakes and make me forget my sorrows and outgrow them; to tell me: there's no such thing as loss! Get up sweetheart!

Dr. Neda says, I know. You have concurrently experienced much pain and loss. After our worst, most fragile experiences, we can become stronger and find deeper meaning in life ... This does not mean that our grief shrinks with the passage of time, but that we are the ones who grow. The worst moments in our lives can be the seeds for the best moments. There are no water lilies without swamps. The prettiest flowers germinate at the heart of the slough. Loss has remarkable power to transform us...

I think the smallest of hopes can at times shake you and make you get up, and this small hope can simply be a word.

I dream that it is mom's funeral but mom is at home.

She lives. She tells me, wear your long overcoat. It suits you. I am standing in front of the mirror and she is watching me admiringly.

I wake up. It's just before five in the morning. I hear mom's voice. Whenever we felt dejected, with strength in her eyes and intensity in her voice, she used to say:

Put your hands on your knees and get up! May these two hands be cut off if they can't carry a head! Get up sweetheart!

Sure mom, I'll get up. And I'd get up! I stand in front of the mirror and stare into my eyes: I know myself. I know what I want from life. Everything is inside me. I won't waste valuable time. I will focus. I will make plans. I will practice. I will love. I will open up my mind. I will stop futile thoughts. I will stop the blame. And I will respect my decision.

Dr. Neda says this is the first step in taking responsibility. You must fully experience sorrow to understand joy.

It warms the cockles of my heart. An inner voice keeps telling me: get up … Words can free a person. Intuition, this inner voice, makes you fly high and peacefully; a long, quiet flight. Intuition exists. Mom is at my side. The world is an enigma. I look up. I watch the flight of birds. They know that the path they are on is the right one. They never deviate. They never get anxious.

Birds are happy. Calm. Content. Satisfied.

The rays of the sun caress my eyes. *Get up Mehraveh!*

I tell myself, wherever there is hope for change, I will follow it. I am a potpourri of all these events, and the gist of it is: giving hope, creating change, falling, and getting back on your feet. I repeat to myself, everything is inside me; you will keep losing until you realize that there is no losing; that in fact, you are simply entering the next stage, and the cycle will continue until you have learned your lesson, grown, understood, and are freed from the trap. *Get up Mehraveh! Everything is inside you!*

When you are completely present, you will begin to see. The whole universe becomes symbols. All its creatures speak to you. You become aware. You wake up. You hear well. You see well. I don't want to lose my focus again. I must concentrate.

The words of a lady who resembles Queen Elizabeth attracts my attention. I came across her videos on YouTube haphazardly. She says: You came here to create ... Fear is not real. Only *love* is real. There are no limitations except for what you construct!

She is Dolores Cannon, the American past-life regressionist and hypnotherapist who treated her patients using the quantum healing hypnosis technique. She made many discoveries and learned information about the previous lives of her patients. I read her books and decide to visit her but I realize that she passed away in October 2014 ... Alas! If only I'd known her sooner.

The disappointment lasts but a few seconds. I find out that Dolores began teaching this method many years ago and her daughter, Julia, has followed in her mother's footsteps. The Quantum Healing Hypnosis Academy has helped treat thousands of people worldwide under her management. I conduct a search on the academy website for the practitioners who were trained by Dolores.

I find Anne Rosart. I visit her website. I search and read more about her. It says: *We learn and evolve as we go through life. Sometimes, we feel that we need guidance and light to keep on the right path. I can help you find the light to achieve many positive changes that you seek. A fantastic journey awaits you and it all starts here!*

I feel I've known her for years. Immediately, I send her an email and can't wait for the answer. After exchanging a few emails, I finally manage to talk to Anne on the phone.

My entire being is filled with an energy that keeps reverberating inside me, telling me that this is the right thing to do; you must go see her; she's the one. Unwittingly, I say that we are constantly recreating ourselves by sending frequencies to the universe.

I light a candle. I connect to the light source. I am totally calmed and I pray:

I am aware that I am in the hands of the eternal power and the divine light. Guide me towards my purpose. Amin.

Anne said that she's booked up until November. She must also spend a day in Ottawa, visiting her mother. She'll checked her diary again.
- How about October 31st? It's Halloween!
- It's fine by me. Let's just do it.
- What have you named your book?
- My mom's name: *Marish*.

I can't stay home. I'm all pulse. The autumn leaves have colored the ground and the trees all around. I walk into a coffee bar. My cell rings. It's Anna.

I say it's crowded in here and I can't hear you.

"I'll make it short. We can meet tomorrow."

I remember seeing a piece of a newspaper underneath my tree. It said in red: *99 soon*.

I laugh. Mom has gathered all the angels around me...

Angel number 99 is the symbol of growth and spiritual awareness. It's a reminder that you are on an important spiritual journey. Seeing this number may mean that you are on the threshold of significant experiences in your spirituality.

How numbers arrive just in time. How their friendship is timely and lasting. Numbers occur at any place, whether on earth or beyond it. Why shouldn't I believe them? They are everywhere. Everything is based on numbers. The movements of the planets, days, nights, months, years, the sky, and the earth ... Numbers are the best medium for sending messages. My angels send these messages; vibrant beings that are the symbol of unconditional love, kindness, and forgiveness. They are connected to the source of life and energy.

In her hypnosis sessions, Dolores Cannon realized that her patients speak to their higher consciousness; the part that goes beyond the corporeal body; the eternal spirit.

I look at the sky. I watch the clouds. I draw a deep breath. I say:

Can you speak to me? Can you accept me? Can you embrace me? Can you tell me what I'm doing here?

I take care not to let anything steal my focus. I get ready for change. I was on the wrong path. I had thrown myself into a vicious circle. I didn't listen. I was stubborn. Now, I feel the inner love and peace. This feeling of love keeps me connected to the source and present in the moment. I close my eyes. Calmness is key. All the fears have surfaced so that I can get rid of them once and for all; so that I can find true energy.

I must be at Anna's place at ten tomorrow morning. She lives in Barrie. It's eighty kilometers from Toronto. Her energy is with me. I don't take my eyes off the sky.

I wear new clothes; I go to see her with a cleansed mind, present with all my heart. I talk to no one. I don't answer any messages. I don't look at my cell. I just keep my eyes on the sky. *Will you accept me?* It says: yes!

But I repeat myself again. I want to be sure. I look at the sky and it says: yes…

I arrive fifteen minutes early. I text Anne and say that I can wait. She writes: come in.

She has a nice bungalow. It is surrounded by trees reaching up to the sky. Maple trees with red leaves make the view of the house even more beautiful.

I go inside. Her dog, Joey, welcomes me. I stroke him.

I say: I'm here Anna. I was meant to come today rather than in three weeks!

She smiles. Her house is filled with light. Magenta leather furniture, white wooden table resembling old chests. There is a wooden tray on the table, filled with healing crystals like amethysts, opals, amazonite… She lights the candle. She has placed two glasses filled with water on the table and tells me, allow me to choose the tea for you; and she brings tea for both of us. We drink some of it. She sips her tea and asks more questions. I trust her. Her silver hair. Her smile. Her kind eyes. I feel like I've known her for a thousand years. I don't feel alienated. Joey sticks to me and sleeps without making a sound. Anne takes notes. She asks: why do you want to experience this journey?

I say I have started asking my higher consciousness to accept me since last night and connect to me, to tell me what it is that I've forgotten. What's my purpose? Why am I here? Am I on the right path? What is it that I am supposed to do? Please allow me to connect to it and find my path…

She asks me about my health. I tell her about the test results and the changes I observe in my immune system every day.

I can't wait for my hypnotherapy session to begin. I am excited but Anne is calm. She says, close your eyes … and she takes me on a short journey. I think that the session has begun but she says no, this was just a test to make you ready. The session takes place on the lower floor of the house.

We go down the stairs.

The basement of her house is also beautiful and filled with pots and plants. Anne uses the hydroponics technique to grow basil, cress, mint, and so on. We go into the room. A very old image of a flying angel is on the wall. A photo of Dolores Cannon is placed in a niche near the ceiling.

There is a light and a heavy blanket on the bed.

Anne asks: which one do you prefer?
- The light one.

I lie down. She pulls the blanket over me and connects my

cell phone to a microphone to record my voice. She presses the video recording button.

- Relax. Speak in any language you like. The entire session will be recorded so that you can listen to it later if you need to and discover some mysteries. I will repeat the questions in English to keep the communication going with you.

There is no music and there is a deadly silence everywhere. Anna's voice has its highs and lows like music notes. She puts a blindfold on my eyes to keep out any environmental distractions.

She utters a few sentences and readies me for the journey. I take a deep breath. I feel like I am breathing with my heart rather than my lungs. I speed away from the American continent towards the west and move away from the planet earth. I don't think it took more than a few seconds. I remember nothing else.

At the end of the session, Anne sends me the video of the hypnotherapy. I watch it and see that it took me a while to start talking! The higher consciousness replies to me with reflection. In fact, it answers Anne's questions. There is a great pain in the back of my head. My face is red. My eyes are open underneath the blindfold but I have no control over my pupils. I feel some intense light every time a plan is approved. It makes me want to close my eyes but I don't even have the strength to blink. The light becomes stronger than I can bear. It is too intense for the body to carry. Objects multiply so that infinite light and love are manifested in various dimensions.

I leave the atmosphere. I have no body. I am nothing. I have no hands, feet, and face. I seem to be a flow of energy. I enter the darkness. Pitch black. Infinity. I float in that absolute darkness. I am alone.

Where are you now Mehi?

- There is complete darkness here. No one is here. There is no fear. They don't allow me out of the darkness!

Who is providing you with this information? Who is not allowing you out?

- I have no idea! I can't see them! I have been punished. I cry.
- They tell me I have no patience; I must learn to wait.

I cry and plead.

- Please … Let me out of here … I am no good in here. There is nothing I can do here. Please!

I ask the higher consciousness to allow Mehi to go somewhere else.

Without fail, I am freed of that darkness.

- It's white everywhere. I seem to be inside a very high, large dome. It has no beginning and no end. There is a bright orb here who is laughing. Oh! Another bright orb comes towards me. They laugh and float up and down. I know these bright orbs. They know me too. They were with me on planet earth. I have known them for very long years. We are playing together.

Are you an orb too?

Silence…

- This place is filled with bright orbs of different sizes. They float up and down. They are all confused. Only my orbs are happy. The rest are confused and annoyed.

Why are they annoyed?
- They have forgotten why they came to earth. The bigger ones have spent a longer time on earth and wasted more time. I am also an orb now.

I become sad.

Why are you there?

Silence...
- There is a higher energy close to me. It is observing us from above. I am not allowed to look at it. It is exalted. My orbs take their orders from it. It seems to be a superior teacher. These two bright orbs are my guides; my guardian angels. One is the size of a basketball and the other is around three times bigger.

We thank the bright orbs for making this meeting possible for you. We bid them farewell and I ask permission from the higher consciousness to take Mehi to the best time and place. We are now there. We stop and watch.

Silence...
- I am in a sandy desert.

What are you wearing? Describe it to me.
- I am walking on the sand but it doesn't scorch. I am wearing a long black dress. I have long black hair and I am wearing a headdress. I am barefoot but my feet don't burn.

Are you wearing any particular jewelery?

Silence...
- I am wearing a very large and heavy silver necklace. I

have a wide bracelet on my left arm.

Do they have a special meaning?
- No.

What do you do there? Do you have a family? Who looks after you?
- I am alone. I have no family. I have a tribe. I am the head of my tribe. I teach them how to live a better life. My tribe respects me. I am a healer. I put herbal balms on their wounds. The men and women of my tribe come to me for help.

Where did you get this knowledge from?
- I don't know. I knew it from before. Everything is inside me. I have been sent here to make life better for my tribesmen.

How do you prepare your food?
- We have many sheep. We have camels. We have rams and goats. We nourish ourselves on the milk and byproducts obtained from the sheep and goats.

Do you have houses?
- We live in tents and migrate from place to place in the desert. Oh! I am in the land of the Arabs.

Let us go to an important day in your life in the land of the Arabs.
- I go mountain climbing at night. I'm afraid of nothing and no one.

What do you do in the mountains? Do you meet someone?
- No. I am alone. I retreat. Something like meditation. I remain silent and I am filled with the answers to my

questions. I seem to be learning.

Who is teaching you?

- There is no one here. I connect to an inner source of energy.

Let us go to another important day in your Arabic life. What do you see?

Long silence…

- It's not clear. Someone is sick. They are suffering. Yes, it's a woman. She is sleeping inside the tent. She is in pain. Her stomach is swollen.

Silence…

I cry…

What's the matter Mehi? Who is that woman?

- That woman looks like my Iranian mother.

I start to sob.

- She is sick. They want me to cure her. I can't. I don't have enough tools.

I cry. I shout. I blame myself.

- I couldn't save your life again.

I wail.

What happened?

- The woman lost her life. There was nothing I could do.

Calm down Mehi. Listen to me. Mehi … Maybe your Arab mother has a message for you.

Silence…

I cry … Silence…

- She says it's not your fault. This was how long my journey lasted. You did everything you could for me. You have been given everything you need beforehand. It is inside you. Your power is love. There is no power higher than love. Love heals everything. Love is a healer. Stop blaming yourself. We experienced another life together so that you can accept that you're blameless. I waited for a long time for you to be born and for me to be your mother. I am happy that you were with me during my last moments in both lives…

I cry.

- My mother carried the weight of this suffering on her shoulders for years and years just to tell me to stop blaming myself. I was given a second chance to forgive myself and let go.

Silence…

- Please let go of me. We each have separate, independent lives. We will meet again on another plane and hug each other. But you won't worry about me again over there. Let go of me, love.

I cry.

Mehi, thank her for giving you this opportunity and message. Forgive yourself. Take your mother in your arms and entrust her to the light and love.

I whisper in a low voice.

- Forgive me … Please forgive me. I don't want you to suffer because of me anymore. I wish you the best of eternal comfort. Be blessed and opulent. Forgive me mother…

We will shut down this image and go to another important day in your Arabic life. What happened to you after you lost her?

I keep blaming myself and can't stay with the tribe anymore. Every time I see my tribesmen, I remember my sin and shortfall. I leave them and die alone.

Let's bring this curtain down and ask the higher consciousness to take Mehi to the best time and place for observation and perception.

Long silence…

- I must learn more. I need to be taught.

Where are you now?

- In a small apartment. Very small. It's full of books. I am in a European country. I have short hair down to my shoulders.

Silence…

- I am in France. In Paris. It's the late 19th century. I am wearing a long, gray raincoat.

What's your objective there? What are your plans?

- I must learn. I am inexperienced. I must learn more.

What's your job?

- I write! I write novels.

Do you have a family? Husband and kids?

- I have some friends but I live alone. I am depressed. I want to end my life.

Do you do it?

- No!

Silence…

I am intrigued to know if you and I meet again.

Silence…

- I am sitting in a wooden café. You're there Anna. We don't know each other. You are a passerby and you ask to share my table. You place your hand over mine. You say you're not going to do this. Everything will be all right.

I cry.

- Anna, you come to me every time I shift from one stage to the next … You leave me with a smile. It is as if we live in parallel worlds at the same time. Your presence indicates that the universe is protecting me. A few days after seeing you, my friends come to my apartment and realize that I have left my body.

I cry nonstop and thank the higher consciousness.

I thank the higher consciousness for sharing this important information with us. We close this page and ask the higher consciousness to scan Mehi's body.

- I see an intense light. They tell me that I am the one who creates any chaos that happens. They give me a clean bill of health. They wash my entire body with light. There are no more blockages.

I cry.

- I have completed my mission. The universe is happy. Everywhere is filled with light. I enter a new stage.

My voice changes.

- And whoever we send to you, be aware and give them help. Love is the answer to all confusions.

There is a great pain in the back of my head. I whisper:

- All this suffering happened to prepare me for this stage. Thank you … Thank you. I promise to be deserving of this reward. Help me not to lose my center again. I will focus. Yes, absolutely. Thank you … I can now return…

Anne thanks the higher consciousness and bids it farewell. She taps on my forehead with her fingers a few times and returns my consciousness to my body in the present time. I am still bewildered. My cheeks are flushed. I feel light.

After visiting Anna, I experience a totally different level of energy. I cannot talk to anyone. I take the cell phone to send a message but I can't. It is as if I am still being updated and receiving new information; like software!

I write. I delete. I am calm and peaceful. I am immersed in myself. I can't even write to Anne to say that her energy is with me and I can feel her. I continue to be enlightened. Concepts are taking shape and becoming clear. My eyes have opened. I hear everything in my head but I don't know how!

My life became tumultuous so that I could remember the main goal and meaning of my life. I had forgotten my main mission on earth. Humans, and forgetfulness and distraction!

Anne sends a message. "A week has passed! I just wanted to know how your week was?"

I write to her, "Your energy hasn't left me for a moment since that day. You are with me and won't leave my thoughts. What baffles me is that I am still putting the pieces of the puzzle together; something like unblocking the blockages in my mind and solving its riddles. It is as if I'm still being updated and acquiring more inner energy … It's beyond belief, I am lost for words…"

I send the message to Anne and get ready to go to the coffee bar near my house. I put my hand on the tree that I love. Every time I put my hand on its trunk, the palm of my hand warms up. This tree is my friend. It seems to send all its energy inside me. I hug it. I say, your orange autumn leaves are very beautiful! They really suit you!

The branch of another tree pulls on my hair. I look up. I laugh. I say I see you too. Hello!

The whole world seems to be dancing and joyful. How could I not have noticed any of it before? The sun comes. I hold my face towards it. I warm up. Its warmth penetrates my entire being.

The image of the custard Danish pastry hasn't left my mind since last night. I go straight to the Pusateri's. I can't believe it. It's out of pastries. Only the kind I wanted is left, and only one of it!

The universe is connected and filled with mysteries. As Hafez said, you are the veil, get up and the path be cleared. And when you get up, everything you see turns into a miracle. It becomes one. It becomes acceptance. Liberation. Forgiveness. It becomes love full stop.

Adam sends me new pictures of the farm. He says: Mehi, we will grow a pennyroyal patch for mother. Bring some magnolia seeds as well, in memory of your mother. We will plant it together at the heart of the farm.

I type:

There are no goodbyes for me mother. Wherever you are, you will always be in my heart.

I draw back the curtains. It's snowing. A year has passed since mom left … I send mom's book to the publishers…

www.ingramcontent.com/pod-product-compliance
Lightning Source LLC
Chambersburg PA
CBHW050208130526
44590CB00043B/3205